L. McWherter

The three Kingdoms

The Kingdom of Heaven, the Kingdom of God and the Father's Kingdom

L. McWherter

The three Kingdoms

The Kingdom of Heaven, the Kingdom of God and the Father's Kingdom

ISBN/EAN: 9783337183974

Printed in Europe, USA, Canada, Australia, Japan

Cover: Foto ©Lupo / pixelio.de

More available books at **www.hansebooks.com**

THE THREE KINGDOMS.

THE KINGDOM OF HEAVEN, THE KINGDOM OF GOD AND THE FATHER'S KINGDOM.

—OR—

THE ORIGIN, IDENTITY, PERPETUITY AND ORDINANCES OF THE

VISIBLE KINGDOM,

WITH ITS RELATIONS TO THE

Invisible and Eternal Kingdoms.

BY REV. L. McWHERTER, B. S.

Pastor C. P. Church, Union City, Tennessee.

UNION CITY, TENN.;
OUR COUNTRY STEAM PRINTING HOUSE,
1883.

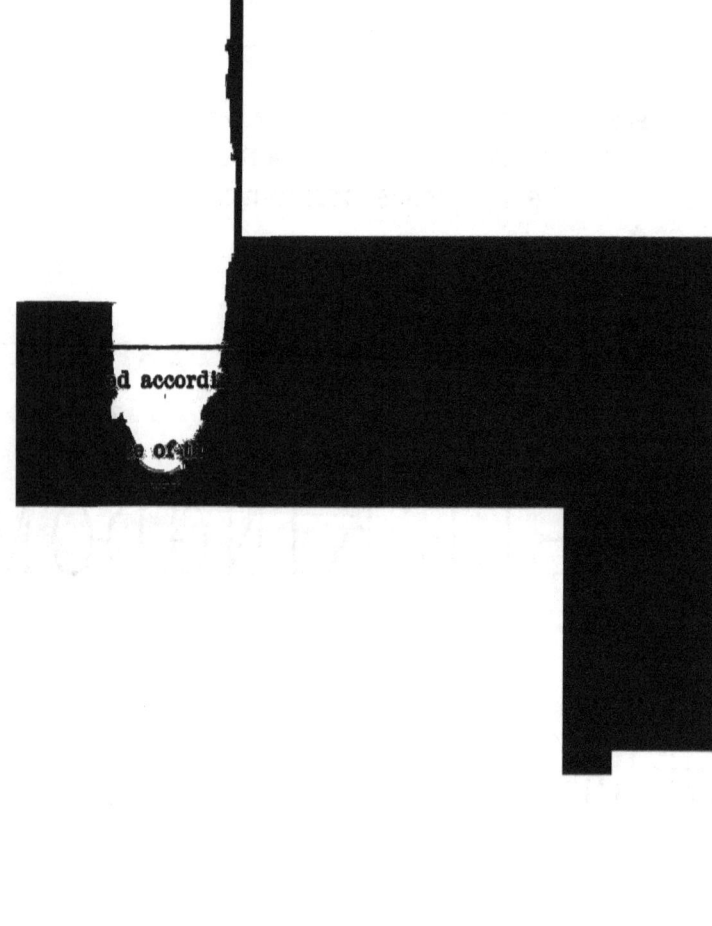

TO
REV. A. B. MILLER, D. D. LL. D.
PRESIDENT OF WAYNESBURG COLLEGE,
WAYNESBURG, PA.

A MAN OF COMPREHENSIVE THOUGHT, MAGNANIMITY OF SOUL AND SWEET SPIRITED DEVOTION TO YOUNG MINISTERS STRIVING TO OBTAIN A LIBERAL EDUCATION, AND FOR YEARS MY HONORED AND MUCH LOVED PRECEPTOR, IS THIS LITTLE VOLUME, WITHOUT CONSULTATION, MOST AFFECTIONATELY DEDICATED BY

THE AUTHOR.

"The kingdoms of this world are become the kingdoms of our Lord and of his Christ."

"In essentials unity,
In non-essentials liberty,
In all things charity."

The loveliest scene—the brightest picture—lost in ultimate and eternal glory.

PREFACE.

We have no apology to make for offering this little volume to the literary, or christian world. In writing it, ALL TRUTH, with NO ERROR, has been our prayer, and *multum in parvo* has been OUR MOTTO. We have made but few references to the original languages, because we desire to be fully comprehended by all who read our little book. It has been our purpose to present plain, scriptural truths, in the clearest possible light. Therefore, we have analyzed carefully the scriptures used, in order to avoid the misapplication of God's word, so common in the discussion of theological questions, and so well calculated to mislead the masses. We have made no special effort at originality of thought, or dress for thought, but have used freely the material brought to our hands through the investigation of others; to all of whom we acknowledge our indebtedness.

Ladened with precious truths, we float this little LIFE-BOAT out upon its heaven-born mission, with deepest solicitude. May it ride triumphantly into the haven, at last, with a CARGO of happy souls on board.

Yours, in hope of Heaven,

L. McWHERTER.

The Kingdom of Heaven.

CHAPTER I.

The Organization of the Visible Church.

Heaven in covenant relation with man, in the organization of the visible kingdom; the union of this visible kingdom with the invisible kingdom, under Christ, David's son and God's Son, and the final submergence of this *dual* kingdom into the glorified kingdom of the Father, is the lovliest scene on earth, the brightest picture on record and the grandest triumph of ultimate and eternal glory.

The church of God is a wonderful phrase, occurs but six times in the Bible, and bears with it a strange, but powerful significance. The church militant, the church spiritual, and the church triumphant, in their three-fold relationship, constitute, in its broadest and most comprehensive sense, the church of God; a division of which is on this side the Jordan of death, while a vast multitude, a grand army, has passed over and pitched their tents on the shores of Immortality.—*One Church and one Owner!*

One God and Father of us all—of whom the whole family (church) in heaven and earth is named. We love this ransomed, blood-bought church of God.

> "I love thy kingdom, Lord,
> The house of thine abode;
> The Church our blest Redeemer saved,
> With His own precious blood.
> I love thy church, O God:
> Her walls before thee stand,
> Dear as the apple of thine eye,
> And graven on thy hand."

The words kingdom and church, as found in the Bible, are often synonymous. They are used interchangably, with the same shade of meaning. By the kingdom of heaven, the inspired writers usually mean the church visible; by the kingdom of God, the church invisible, and by the Father's kingdom, the church glorified. In the kingdom of heaven we have among the king's guests, a man without the wedding garment, the tares mixed with the wheat; the bad fishes in the same net with the good; the foolish virgins in company with the wise; the unfaithful servants along with the faithful, and Judas, "a devil from the beginning," associated with the other apostles; or, in other words, we have the self-deceived, hypocrits and genuine christians, all mixed and mingled together in the church visible. Sad state indeed! Would to God we could spare our much loved Zion the shame and disgrace thus heaped upon her, and heaven itself the melting tear of blasted hope.

The visible church is a body of people separated from the world, for God's service, with ordinances of divine appointment, and a door of entrance by which membership is recognized. This visible church has a visible membership. This constitutes its visibility. Its membership is neither invisible nor spiritual; is not composed of the spirits, or souls of mankind, but wholly of their bodies. Joining the church then does not, as some claim, effect, or change, the relation of the soul to God. Church membership is no evidence of regeneration. Christ said in this connection: The kingdom of heaven is like unto a net, that was cast into the sea and gathered of every kind: which when it was full, they drew to shore, and set down, and gathered the good into vesels, but cast the bad away. He also compared the visible church to a field containing wheat and tares; but said, Let both grow together until the harvest: and in the time of the harvest I will say to the reapers, Gather ye together first the tares, and bind them in bundles to burn them; but gather the wheat into my barn. And then added, in interpreting the parable, So shall it be in the end of the world. The Son of man shall send forth his angels, and they shall gather out of his kingdom all things that offend, and them which do iniquity, and shall cast them into a furnace of fire: there shall be wailing and gnashing of teeth. Then shall the righteous shine forth as the sun in the kingdom of their Father—the glorified kingdom. "Therefore is the kingdom of heaven likened unto a certain king, which would take account of his servants."

But we say the visible church has a door of entrance by which membership is recognized. But water baptism is not that door; spiritual baptism is not that door; neither is Christ himself that door. The official representatives, who receive individuals into the visible church, constitute that door. Through this door only can we pass in, and become *bona fide* members of the visible kingdom. But when and where was this visible church organized? We are all agreed that there is a visible organization, or compact, called the church of God. We are doubtless also agreed, that it is of divine origin; was organized after the creation of man, and for man. If the visible church be of divine origin, and for man, then we claim that it must have been brought into existence by, under, or in persuance of a covenant, entered into between God and man. Why? Because

God deals with men, in a formal way, only through covenants. A covenant, properly speaking, is simply an agreement, a contract, a bargain between two parties. But when one party is infinitely superior to the other, as in a contract between God and man, then the covenant assumes the nature of a promise; sometimes conditional, and sometimes unconditional, as we will see further on. We wish to state just here, and would have it remembered, that our God is not only a covenant-making, but also a covenant-keeping God. For his covenants are not made to be broken; and his promises are all yea and amen in Christ Jesus.

We will now examine the covenants briefly, in search of the origin of the visible church; and see if possible in which of these covenants the visible kingdom had its birth. We wish to say first however, that God never does anything that might as well not be done; nor does he leave undone anything that had better be done, God makes no mistakes of this kind. Hence, we argue that he had a special design, or purpose, in every covenant he made with man. These purposes will be brought to light as we proceed to investigate this subject.

We begin with the first, or ADAMIC COVENANT. "And the Lord God commanded the man, saying, Of every tree of the garden thou mayest freely eat: But of the tree of the knowledge of good and evil, thou shalt not eat of it; for in the day that thou eatest thereof thou shalt surely die," or, in the original, dying thou shalt die. You see at once that there is no reference to the organization of a church in this covenant. The fact is, Adam was pure and holy, and the object of the covenant seemed to be, to secure continued obedience upon his part. Adam was the representative, under this covenant, of human nature as a unit, a single thing. He broke this covenant and fell; and human nature fell with his fall. And so, he rendered perfect obedience to his posterity, an impossibility; and God never has and never will make another covenant with man for that specific purpose.

THE COVENANT WITH NOAH is the second in order. "And God spake unto Noah, and to his sons with him, saying, And I, behold, I establish my covenant with you, and with your seed after you; and with every living creature that is with you, of the fowl, of the cattle, and of every beast of the earth with you; from all that go out of the ark, to every beast of the earth. And I will establish my covenant with you; neither shall all flesh be cut off any more by the waters of a flood; neither shall there any more be a flood to destroy the earth. And God said, This is the token of the covenant which I make between me and you and every living creature that is with you, for perpetual generations. I do set my bow in the cloud, and it shall be for a token of a covenant between me and the earth. And it shall come to pass, when I bring a cloud over the earth, that the bow shall be seen in the cloud: and I will remember my covenant, which is between me and you and every living creature of all flesh; and the waters shall no more become a flood to destroy all flesh. And the bow shall be in the cloud; and I will look upon it, that I may remember the everlasting covenant between God and every living creature of all flesh that is upon the earth. And God said unto Noah, This is the token of the covenant, which I have established between me and all flesh that is upon the earth." Still we have no mention of a church. The object of this covenant was to secure the world against the unnecessary fear of another flood. And the token of its fulfillment is the bow in the cloud. Beautiful rainbow! A coronet on the brow of the gathering storm, spanning the blackening heavens with the sun-light of hope—an everlasting token of God's glorious promise to the wide, wide world, that there shall be no more flood, but fruitful years to bless the earth, while time shall roll her annals round. Neither will God ever make another covenant for this specific purpose.

THE LAND COVENANT comes next. "In the same day the Lord made a covenant with Abram, saying, Unto thy seed have I given this land, from the river of Egypt unto the great river, the river Euphrates." Not the slightest reference to the organization of the church as yet. The object of this covenant was simply to insure Abram though eighty-four years old, and childless, that his seed should inherit the promised land. Abram, high father, or father of one nation, whose seed should be as the dust of the earth and as the stars of heaven for multitude, accepted the promise and died in the triumps of a living faith. God remembered his covenant, verified his promise, and Abram's posterity inherited the promised land. But God will never make another covenant for this specific purpose.

THE SINAIC COVENANT is the fifth in regular order. "And Moses went up unto God, and the Lord called unto him out of the mountain, saying, Thus shalt thou say to the house of Jacob, and tell the children of Israel; ye have seen what I did unto the Egyptians, and how I bear you on eagles' wings, and brought you unto myself. Now therefore, if ye will obey my voice indeed, and keep my covenant, then ye shall be a peculiar treasure unto me above all people: for all the earth is mine: and ye shall be unto me a kingdom of priests, and an holy nation. And the Lord said unto Moses, Write thou these words: for after the tennor of these words I have made a covenant with thee and with Israel. And he was there with the Lord forty days and forty nights; he did neither eat bread, nor drink water. And he wrote upon the tables the words of the covenant, the ten commandments." This is the substance of the law covenant, made at Mount Sinai after Moses brought Israel out from that dark night of Egyptian bondage. The church was now in existence, and called the "congregation of Israel." She had her ordinances, circumcision and the Passover, already instituted. She also had her elders, and her ministers; the priests with divers laws, and minor ordinances, that God had given her. Moses gathered together all the elders of the children of Israel, instituted the holy priesthood and clothed the Lord's ministers with garments excellent "for glory and for beauty." God speaks of Israel in this connection as "My people." And Luke refers to her, at this period as "the church in the wilderness." So the visible church was, at this eppoc, beyond all doubt a creature of existence. And yet there is not a word said in this covenant about its organization. Then it must have been brought into being somewhere between this and the land covenant, for it had no existence prior to, nor, was it brought into existence under that covenant. It is competent to say then, that we may hope to find, yea, that we will *most certainly* find, the origin of this visible church in the fourth covenant.

THE COVENANT OF PROMISE is the fourth in regular order. Here, we claim, is found divine authority for, and the actual organization of the visible church. And if here, then, with due deference to the opinion of others, allow me to say, nowhere else; for there is no reference, anywhere in the Bible, to the organization, or existence of a new or second visible church of God. But this covenant is lengthy and we will only give it in substance. "And when Abram was ninety years old and nine, the Lord appeared to Abram, and said unto him, I am the Almighty God; walk before me, and be thou perfect. And I will make my covenant between me and thee, and will multiply thee exceedingly. Behold my covenant is with thee, and thou shalt be a father of many nations. Neither shall thy name any more be called Abram, but thy name shall be Abraham; for a father of many nations have I made thee. And I will make thee exceeding fruitful; and establish my covenant between me and thee and thy seed after thee in their generations for an everlasting covenant. This is my covenant, which ye shall keep; every man child among you shall be circumcised; and it shall be a token of the covenant betwixt me and you. He that is eight days old shall be circumcised, every man child in your generations, he that is born in the house, or bought with money of any stranger: and my covenant (the sign of my covenant) shall be in your flesh for an evertasting covenant. As for Sarai thy wife, thou shalt not call her name Sarai, but Sarah: and I will bless her and she shall be a mother of nations. Sarah thy wife shall bear thee a son indeed; and thou shalt call his name Isaac: and I will establish my covenant with him for an everlasting covenant, and with his seed after him. And as for Ishmael, I have heard thee: Behold, I have blessed him, and will make him fruitful and multiply him exceedingly; but my covenant will I establish with Isaac." In the selfsame day Abraham, his son and all the men of his house were circumcised, we are told.

Now we have found the origin of the visible church — the germ of the church, the church in embrio, the miniature church, organized in the family of the grand old patriarch, Abraham. This organization occured about nineteen hundred years before Christ. Abram high-father, or father of one nation, is now changed to Abraham, high-father of many nations; and Sarai my princess, to Sarah princess, or mother of nations. And the little germ church, watered with heaven's richest dews, began to develop and grow; the embryonic kingdom gradually lengthened her cords and strengthened her stakes, as the mighty sweep of centuries rolled away into the dim vista of by-gone ages, and at length the kingdom of heaven came forth, in her conquering glory, a mighty host, "fair as the moon, clear as the sun and terrible as an army with banners."

CHAPTER II.

THE IDENTITY OF THE VISIBLE CHURCH.

Our object, in this and the next chapter, is to identify the visible church under the old and new dispensations. For, strange as it may seem, some claim that the church is not identical under these two dispensations; but that the old church died with the old dispensation, and that a *new church* was born with the new dispensation, the Bible to the contrary notwithstanding.

To fix the exact date of the organization of this *would be* new church, or to agree as to the place of its birth, has given our friends no small amount of trouble. Some of them locate its, supposed, origin "about the time of John the Baptist," some, "during the ministry of Christ," others, "on the day of Penticost," and still others, "somewhere along there under a new covenant." We submit, if any of these suppositions be true, would not some record of, or reference to, such organization of said new church be found in the New Testament? But we have no such record, or reference. The inference is conclusive, if such a church exist,

Christ did not organize it; nor did he authorize the apostles so to do.

But still the advocates of this theory claim that the Jewish church was dissolved and a new church reared upon its ruins. They contend that the Scriptures clearly teach that this, supposed, wonderful revolution in ecclesiastical history occured somewhere about the ushering in of the Christian era. Yet they fail to agree as to when, and where, the old church, as they called it, breathed its last, and their new church first immersed itself in the pure atmostphere of heaven, and threw open wide its doors to the children of men. Even their leading men differ widely on this question. Yes, their "brightest lights" send forth rays as divergent as the beams of light that find their way from the king of day to the opposite poles of *terra firma*. For instance, Mr. Mell, in his work on Baptism, says, "The new church was organized on the day of Penticost." With this statement Mr. Crowell, Cramp and Orchard all agree. But Mr. Peay enters his protest, and says, "The new church was organized by the Saviour on the mountain," where he ordained the twelve apostles, that he might send them forth to preach, heal the sick and cast out devils. But Mr. Dayton says, "The new church was organized by John the Baptist in the river Jordan." Strange place indeed to organize a church! But to cap the climax, and throw all "lesser lights" completely in the shade, Mr. Howell says, "The new church had its birth in the upper room, on the night of the betrayal." How remarkably strange that all his brethren cannot see it in the same light! For he adds, she arose, then and there, "as bright as the morning sun without a cloud." We submit; does this not look a little too much like guess work, even among these "bright lights" of the new church theory? "If a kingdom be divided against itself that kingdom shall fall." But still they hold their ground, diversified as are their opinions, and challenge the world to the enormous task of overthrowing this baseless fabric—the "new church" theory. They refer us to scriptures which they claim prove their positions, and ask, at our hands, their prayerful consideration. We shall now examine a few of the most important of these scriptures, and show how far they are from establishing the "new church" theory.

Daniel says, in interpreting Nebuchadnezzar's dream, "And in the days of these kings shall the God of heaven set up a kingdom, which shall never be destroyed; and the kingdom shall not be left to other people, but it shall break in pieces and consume all these kingdoms, and it shall stand forever." This, they regard as one of their strongest holds. We must understand the dream in order to understand this verse in the interpretation. The great image, was some of the most prominent kingdoms of this world; and the stone that "smote the image, became a great mountain, and filled the whole earth" was the church organized in the household of Abraham, which had fallen down and trailed her banner in the dust. But this dilapidated, down-fallen, world-ridden, sorely persecuted church was the visible kingdom that the God of heaven proposed to *set up* again in the midst of her enemies, and cause to stand forever. In the days of these kings shall the God of heaven *set up* a kingdom. Mark the words, *set up*; not organize, create or bring into existence something new; a "new church" for instance; but *set up* something that already existed—that grand old visible kingdom, that shall have no end, that shall break in pieces and cosume all other kingdoms, be submerged at last in the kingdom of eternal glory and stand forever and forever.

The setting up of this kingdom was simply the raising up of the tabernacle of David that had fallen down. This visible kingdom is often spoken of as a tabernacle. David inquired of the Lord, to know, who should abide in this tabernacle, or who should remain members of this visible church, when Christ should come to re-establish it under a new covenant. And the answer was, He that walketh uprightly and worketh righteousness, and speaketh the truth in his heart. In other words, only the righteous. God was evidently speaking of his visible kingkom when he said through the prophet Jeremiah; My tabernacle is spoiled, and all my cords are broken: my children are gone forth of me, and they are not: there is none to stretch forth my tent any more, and to set up my curtains. For the pastors are become brutish, and have not sought the Lord; therefore they shall not prosper, and all their flocks shall be scattered. God also spoke of the restoration of this same kingdom to its former glory, when he said by the mouth of his prophet Amos: In that day will I raise up the tabernacle of David that is fallen, and close up the breaches thereof; and I will raise up his ruins, and I will build it as in the days of old. Or, as in Isaiah: And in mercy shall the throne be established: and he (Christ) shall sit upon it in truth in the tabernacle of David, judging, and seeking judgment, and hasting righteousness. And the key of the house of David will I lay up on his shoulder; so he shall open, and none shall shut, and he shall shut, and none shall open. In perfect harmony with the above, is the language of James, in defense of Paul and Barnabas, by whom God had wrought such miracles among the Gentiles. He says: And to this agree the words of the prophets; as it is written, After this I will return, and will build again the tabernacle of David, which is fallen down; and I will build again the ruins thereof, and I will set it up: that the residue of men might seek after the Lord, and all the Gentiles, upon whom my name is called. This passage shows clearly that we did not mislay these prophecies. We find no organization of a "new church" here; but simply the setting up again of that visible kingdom that had been broken down—the rebuilding of the tabernacle of David that was now to stand forever. This reference to the visible kingdom, in its fallen down condition, as a tabernacle, is perfectly naturally, since the tabernacle of Moses was so constructed as to be taken down and set up again at pleasure.

Another scripture upon which they rely is this: And I say also unto thee, That thou art Peter, (*petros*) and upon this rock (*Petra*) I will build my church; and the gates of hell shall not prevail against it. We must be able to analyze scripture before we can hope to understand it. Before this passage can avail the advocates of the "new church" theory anything, they will have to prove that the church founded upon the Rock Christ Jesus, is the visible, and not the spiritual kingdom. This they cannot do. For Peter himself says, If so be ye have tasted that the Lord is gracious, to whom coming, as unto a living stone, disallowed indeed of men, but chosen of God, and precious, ye also, as lively stones, are built up a spiritual house, a holy priesthood, to offer up spiritual sacrifices, acceptable to God by Jesus Christ. Here is the spiritual church—the kingdom of God, "the spiritual house" founded upon the Rock Christ Jesus. But Paul also adds his testimony upon this point: Now therefore ye are no more strangers and foreigners, but fellow-citizens with the saints, and of the household of God; and are built upon the foundation of the apostles and prophets, Jesus Christ himself being the chief cornerstone; in whom all the building fitly framed together, groweth unto a holy temple in the Lord; in whom ye also are builded together, for a habitation of God through the Spirit. Now we see, that the church built upon the Rock, was not the visible, but the spiritual kingdom, the kingdom of God, "the household of God," "a holy temple fitly framed together," not by man, as is the visible church, but by the Holy Spirit, the architect of this spiritual kingdom. We submit this proposition to our opponents on this question. When do you regard converts on the "Rock of ages"? When are their feet firmly planted on the sure foundation of the apostles and prophets? When do they sing with the spirit and with the understanding, He hath taken my feet out of the miry clay and set them upon the Rock, and he hath put a new song in my mouth, even praise unto our God? Is it when they become members of the visible, or when they are born into the spiritual kingdom? All, with one accord, unless they have adopted the dogma of "baptismal regeneration," and believe that water baptism is the door into both, the spiritual and visible church, must answer, when they are born of God, born of the Spirit, born into the spiritual kingdom—the kingdom of God. Then the question is settled. The scripture under consideration has no reference to the visible, but to the invisible, the spiritual church, our opponents themselves being the judges.

The last passage that we shall notice upon which they rely is this: The law and the prophets were until John: since that time the kingdom of God is preached, and every man presseth into it. Here it is self-evident that the spiritual, and not the visible, church is meant.

John's was most emphatically a spiritual ministry—a ministry of repentance and faith. To the self-righteous Pharisees and self-conceited Sadducees, who came to his baptism, he said, O generation of vipers, who hath warned you to flee from the wrath to come? Bring forth teerefore fruits meet for repentance. I indeed baptize you with water unto repentance: but he that cometh after me is mightier than I: he shall baptize you with the Holy Ghost and with fire. And he came into all the country about Jordan, preaching the baptism of repentance for (in order to) the remission of sins. There was a man sent from God whose name was John, the same came for a witness, to bear witness of the Light, that all men through him might believe. And pointing to this Light he is saying to men to-day, Behold, (with the eye of faith) the Lamb of God which taketh away the sin of the world. The kingdom that John preached then, was the same that Jesus preached when he came into Galilee, after that John was put in prison, preaching the gospel of the kingdom of God, and saying, the time is fulfilled and the kingdom of God is at hand; repent ye and believe the gospel. The same that Jesus preached when he went throughout every city and vilage preaching and showing the glad tidings of the kingdom of God. The same that his disciples preached when he sent them to preach the kingdom of God, and to heal the sick. This is the kingdom that Christ preached to Nichodemus when he said, Verily, verily, I say unto thee, except a man be born again he cannot see the kingdom of God. For, says Christ, the kingdom of God is not meat and drink, but righteousness and peace and joy in the Holy Ghost. This is the kingdom that has been preached since the days of John the Baptist and into which so many pressed. Shame on the minister that would forsake the spiritual, to preach the visible kingdom; that would leave the substance for the shadow. Then John preached the kingdom of God, the spiritual kingdom; and the people pressed into it, insomuch that it is said, the kingdom suffered violence and the violent took it by force. This strong and impressive language simply indicates the anxiety, and difficulty, with which soul-burdened and heart-bleeding penitents forced their way, amid tears, prayers and supplications, into this spiritual kingdom. It is a very easy matter to get into the visible, but by no means a pleasant task to press one's way into the spiritual kingdom. This requires effort, sacrifice, repentance, godly sorrow, a turning away from sin and a looking up to Christ. The church refered to then, in the passage now under consideration, is the spiritual and not the visible by any means.

If time permitted we might notice other passages, from which they argue the organization of a "new church," with the same, or similar results. The above will have to suffice however as a specimen of their logic on this subject. The misapplication of these passages show conclusively that their cause is sorely pressed, when they search the Scriptures in proof of the organization of a "new church."

The identity of the visible church, under the old and new dispensations, does not, as they claim, involve absurdities and impossibilities. These supposed absurdities and impossibilities take the wings of the wind, or like the mists of the morning, melt away before the rising sun of truth. If our opponents were not blind to the distinction that exists between the visible and spiritual kingdoms, in their zeal to organize a new church, they would not find so many difficulties, in reconciling the identity of the visible kingdom, with the ushering in of a new dispensation—the introduction of a new era in the history of the church and the world. It is, and always has been, one thing to be a member of the visible, but quite a different thing to be born into, or become identified with the spiritual church. Men of the blackest hearts, sometimes belong to the visible kingdom; while purity of heart is absolutely indispensible to recognition in the spiritual kingdom. The Scribes and Pharisees who clamored for the blood of the Just One, and Judas who betrayed innocent blood for thirty pieces of silver, with the multitude that cried, Away with this man, crucify him! crucify him! all belonged to the visible church. But who would have the audacity to say that any of them were identified with the spiritual kingdom, which Christ said the unrighteous should not inherit. And yet this is just what they virtually do, who deny what they are pleased to call "the supposed identity of the Jewish church, and the Christian church." There is but one visible, one spiritual, and will be but one glorified church.

CHAPTER III.

THE IDENTITY OF THE VISIBLE CHURCH.

OUR FIRST ARGUMENT on the identity of the visible church is based on the *new covenant.* That God made a new covenant, with a certain people, at the introduction of the Christian dispensation, all are agreed. And if a *new* church was organized "about that time," by divine authority, it must, of *necessity,* have been inpersuance of this covenant; for there was no other under which it could have been brought into existence. But to whom was the covenant made? Here we differ, and differ widely. The advocates of the "new church" theory say, to the new, or Christian church. We say, to the old, or Jewish church, organized in the family of Abraham. But to decide this question we must go to "the law and the testimony." God speaks through the mouth of Jeremiah the prophet: Behold, the days come, saith the Lord, that I will make a new covenant with the house of Israel, and with the house of Judah: not according to the covenant that I made with their fathers in the day that I took them by the hand to bring them out of the land of Egypt; which my covenant they brake, although I was a husband to them, saith the Lord: but this shall be the covenant that I will make with the house of Israel after those days, saith the Lord: I will put my law in their inward parts, and write it in their hearts; and I will be their God, and they shall be my people. And they shall teach no more every man his neighbor, and every man his brother, saying, Know the Lord: for they shall all know me, from the least of them unto the greatest of them, saith the Lord: for I will forgive their iniquity, and I will remember their sin no more. Does this look like God intended to authorize the organization of a new church, under this covenant, when he says, *most positively, with the house of Israel, and with the house of Judah?* Yes—yes—we know he said he would make it with the house of Israel, and with the house of Judah, but—but—he did not do it; say the advocates of the "new church" theory. If you expect us to believe what you say, you will have to prove it from the New Testament. Alright: God spoke to the Hebrews, in the broad sunlight of the Gospel dispensation, by the noted apostle Paul, saying of Christ, He is the mediator of a better covenant, which was established upon better promises. For if that first covenant (the

Sinaic) had been faultless, then should no place have been sought for the second. For finding fault with them he saith, Behold the days come, saith the Lord, when I will make a new covenant—with a new church? No, no, not that; but, *with the house of Israel, and with the house of Judah.* He continues to quote, almost verbatim, the entire covenant. Where is your new church? Does this look like God had swept out of existence, that grand old church that he planted with his own hands in the family of Abraham, watered and nourished for centuries in the house of Israel and the house of Judah, and erected a new church upon its ruins, into which, simply a few of the proselyted Jews were permitted to come? Not much like it, I must say. Because the law, or Sinaic covenant, waxed old and vanished away, and God placed the church under this new covenant of grace, "a better covenant established upon better promises," our opponents wildly jumped to the conclusion that it was the visible church that "waxed old and vanished away," and hence, that a new church was of necessity organized, no matter if there was no provision for such organization in this new covenant, or divine authority, for such procedure to be found between the lids of the Holy Bible.

OUR SECOND ARGUMENT on this subject is founded on the testimony of Christ, as recorded by Matthew. In this testimony the Saviour carries the church over grandly, from the old to the new dispensation. In rather a lengthy parable he condemned the Jews, as "wicked husbandmen" who had beaten, stoned and killed God's prophets, and his Son, and withheld the fruits of his vineyard—the church. Out of their own mouths he forced the verdict of guilty. When the lord therefore of the vineyard cometh, what will he do unto those husbandmen? They say unto him, He will miserably destroy those wicked men, and will let out his vineyard unto other husbandmen, which shall render him the fruits in their seasons. Jesus saith unto them, therefore say I unto you, The kingdom of God shall be taken from you, (as a nation) and given to a nation bringing forth the fruits thereof. Does this testimony savor much of the organization of a new church? No! It rather looked to the reformation, or purifying, of the then existing church. If we take the evidence of men and of angels, the evidence of Christ is *infinitely* greater; and Christ has thus testified to the identity of God's visible church, under the Jewish and Gospel dispensations.

OUR THIRD ARGUMENT relative to church

identity, rests upon the apostle Paul's testimony, to the Romans, on this subject. He says, the promise that Abraham should be the heir of the world, was not to him, or his seed through the law, but through the righteousness of faith. Or, to paraphrase: this precious promise that gave Abraham the assurance that he should stand at the head of the church, born in his own household, as its recognized father, in all ages of the world, came not in consequence of perfect obedience rendered to the Sinaic, or law, covenant, but in anticipation of the new covenant of grace, which lit up his soul, with the star-light of hope, as he beheld it a far off, with the sleepless eye of faith. For if they which are of the law be heirs, faith is made void, and the promise made of none effect. Therefore it is of faith, that it might be by grace; to the end the promise might be sure to all the seed which is of the faith of Abraham, who is the father of us all. Who against hope believed in hope, that he might become the father of many nations; he staggered not at the promise of God through unbelief; but was strong in faith, giving glory to God. Thus *all-conquering grace,* though seen through the promise afar off, while sojourning from place to place a stranger in a strange land, dwelling in tabernacles with

Isaac and Jacob, the heirs with him of the same promise, lulled the fears of this grand old Patriarch to sleep, with the sweet melody of faith, while gently reclining his hoary head on the downy pillow of hope. For he looked for a city which hath foundations, whose builder and maker is God.

But again, in perfect harmony with the above, he says to the Gentiles: For if the first fruit be holy, the lump is also holy: and if the root be holy, so are the branches. And if some of the branches be broken off, and thou, being a wild olive-tree, wert graffed in among them, and with them partakest of the root and fatness of the olive tree; boast not against the branches. But if thou boast thou bearest not the root, but the root thee. Thou wilt say then, The branches were broken off, that I might be graffed in. Well; because of unbelief they were broken off, and thou standest by faith. And they also, if they abide not still in unbelief, shall be graffed in: for God is able to graff them in again. For if thou wert cut out of the olive-tree which is wild by nature, and wert graffed contrary to nature into a good olive-tree; how much more shall these, which be the natural branches, be graffed into their own olive-tree? Can you see anything in this testimony of the great apostle to the Gentiles that gives the mere semblance of shelter, or umbrage, to the "new church" theory? And yet the advocates of this theory (more unreasonable than the Romans) would have us believe that the good olive-tree of the Jews, the Jewish church, has been literally destroyed, body, branches, root and all, and that the wild olive-tree of the Gentiles has become the Christian church, under the Gospel dispensation. Strange logic indeed to set up beside these inspired truths which teach us so clearly that the church under the two dispensations is one and the same church.

OUR FOURTH ARGUMENT, in favor of church identity, is grounded upon the following scriptural truths:

First truth. Christ was in the visible church under the old dispensation as well as the new. Our opponents would have us believe that the Jewish church, as they call it, was a Christless church. But not so; Christ was the very heart of the promise made to Abraham, in persuance of which the church was organized in his household. Christ is the *alpha* and *omega* of the church, whether under the Jewish or Gospel dispensation. He is its everlasting foundation; its solid comfort; its anchored hope; its underlying principle; its cardinal truth; its almighty power; and other foundation can no man lay than that is laid, which is Christ Jesus the Lord. He is the Rock of Ages upon which the church was built. Paul says the blessing of Abraham came on the Gentiles through Jesus Christ, that they might receive the promise of the Spirit through faith; and that the promise was made to Abraham and his seed, which is Christ. Then truly if ye be Christ's, then are ye also Abraham's seed. He also told the brethren, that the Jewish fathers, all ate the same spiritual meat, that they ate; and did all drink the same spiritual drink that they drank: for they drank of that spiritual Rock that followed the church through the wilderness; and that *Rock was Christ*. Strange argument indeed. I fail to comprehend it: Christ, the foundation, the meat, the drink, the very heart of a Christless church? No! the church never was without a Christ. Christ was the Rock from which the church was hewn: her strong Rock; her Rock and fortress; the Rock that poured her out rivers of oil; the Great Rock that overshadowed her as she journeyed in a weary land. No wonder then, that the church sang in the lofty strains of the sweet singer of Israel, Lead me to the Rock that is higher than I.

Second truth. The gospel was preached in the church under the old dispensation. Paul says, The Scripture foreseeing that God would justify the heathen through faith, preached the gospel before unto Abraham, saying, In thee shall all the nations of the earth be blessed. I fail to understand, how all the nations of the earth are to be blessed in Abraham, if he be not the father of the *one church,* that God had ladened with blessings for all the world.

Third truth. The organic law of the church remains the same under the new covenant, or gospel dispensation. True the burdensome ceremonies of the Levitical law were abrogated. Paul says, Christ blotted out the hand writing against us, nailing it to his cross: that he abolished the enmity, existing between the Jews and Gentiles, even the law of commandments contained in ordinances, that he might reconcile both unto God in one body by the cross. The symbols and types were changed; a few simple, but significant ordinances were substituted instead of the seremonial law, but the organic law of the church remained ever the the same. The moral code, or decalogue, was boiled down and embodied in the two great commandments; and the doors of the church, hitherto confined to the Jewish nation, thrown open wide enough to receive the whole Gentile world. The apostles were devinely commissioned to go out and preach the gospel of this kingdom to all the nations of the earth. Christ did not authorize them to organize a new church, but simply to extend the borders of the *already existing church*. In the impressive language of his servant Isaiah, the Master sent them out to enlarge the tent of the Jew, to stretch forth the curtain of his habitation, to lengthen his cords, strengthen his stakes, and cause him to inherit the Gentile world. This looks very much to me like the visible church had remained, *one and the same, identical kingdom, both under the Jewish, and Gentile dispensation*.

OUR FIFTH ARGUMENT is designed to prove and illustrate *the oneness, sameness, or indentity of the vissible church* through the political identity of our commonwealth. Is the commonwealth of Tennessee the same commonwealth it was forty years ago? Certainly it is, you answer. How do you know, I ask? Have not the people and laws both changed? Yes, you answer; but the *constiution,* the *organic law*, of the state is the same; and the *governing power* is the same; *the sovereign people still reign*, and this is enough to constitute the idenitity of our grand old commonwealth as long as she continues to be a commonwealth, and float her proud banner out upon the balmy breezes of the benignant heavens. So with the church militant; she has outlived many generations, and witnessed many changes in her statutes, but her *grand old constitution,* her *organic law* —supreme love to God and pure love to man —remain always, and forever, the same, and *the same eternal King reigns eternally:* and this is enough to constitute the *oneness, sameness, or identity* of the now visible, but hereafter glorified kingdom of God through all ages, under all dispensations, in time, and throughout boundless eternity.

OUR SIXTH ARGUMENT, to settle at once, and forever, the subject of church identity, is built upon the Revelator's wonderful vision of the glorified church. While in the spirit on the isle of Patmos the Revelator saw the holy Jerusalem, the glorified church, descending out of heaven from God. He saw her massive walls and gates of pearl, with the names of the twelve tribes of the children of Israel written upon them in letters of gold, while upon its garnished walls of precious stones he beheld engravened the names of the twelve apostles of the Lamb. Glorious vision indeed! The Bride in all her beauty, loveliness and glory, adorned for her husband. Come hither, said the angel to John, and I will show thee the bride, the Lamb's wife. Now John, behold the Bride! far more glorious than when Solomon said, She is the fairest among women, her cheeks comely with rows of jewels, her neck ornamented with chains of gold, all fair, beautified and comely as Jerusalem, while with her attendant queens and virgins she rested under his banner of love. Now she is *glorified;* decked with the ornaments of *redeeming, sanctifying, glorifying grace,* and robed with the beautiful garments of *righteousness,* she stands beside the Lamb on mount Sion and with a voice as the voice of many waters she sings the new song of redeeming grace. Patriarchs, prophets, apostles, Jews and Gentiles join in this grand, triumphant chorus, and thus consumate forever the *oneness, unity and identity of God's visible kingdom.*

CHAPTER IV.

The Perpetuity of the Visible Church.

Our first argument in favor of the perpetuity of the visible church, is supported by the covenant in persuance of which it was brought into existence. We argue that the continuation of the covenant demands the perpetuity of the church. It is unreasonable to suppose that the church would cease to exist sooner than the covenant. But how long was the covenant to stand good? How long was it to endure? *Forever.* It was to be *an everlasting covenant.* Why? Because it was a contract, or covenent, entered into between God and a church that was to know no end; a visible kingdom that will endure the ravages of time, in the end be delivered up by the Son to the Father, and, in its glorified state, go on parallel with God and with eternity. But we will let the sweet singer of Israel talk to you awhile on this subject; O ye seed of Abraham, his servant, ye children of Jacob his chosen. He is the Lord our God; his judgments are in all the earth. He hath remembered his covenant forever, the word which he commanded to a thousand generations. Which covenant he made with Abraham, and his oath unto Isaac; and confirmed the same unto Jacob for a law, and to Israel for an everlasting covenant. How long does God propose to remember his covenant to Israel—the visible church? *Forever.* How long did God command the word of his covenant to stand with this visible kingdom? Through *a thousand generations.* Now, if our friends will just have the kindness to wait until *forever* comes to an end, or, even until *a thousand generations,* of this grand old visible kingdom, organized under this *everlasting covenant,* have been numbered with the past, then they can organize their new church if they wish. But there were nine hundred and fifty seven of these generations yet to follow, on the day of Pentecost; or over forty. thousand years yet to be numbered with the past before they dare set about this unnecessary work. It is to be hoped that they will see the folly of organizing a new church and change their minds before the thousaand generations have passed. This is *a wonderful covenant* that God *made* with Abraham, *renewed,* with an oath, unto Isaac; and *confirmed* unto Jacob for a law, and to Israel for an everlasting covenant, if it ceased to be, and its offspring, *the church,* died with the expiring agonies of the old dispensation. *Such is not true.*

OUR SECOND ARGUMENT, on the perpetuity of the church, is made in the light of God's covenant with David. Saul was the first king, or captain, of Israel. He was chosen by the people, but never anointed of God: for he did evil, displeased the Lord and the Lord rejected him; saying, I have provided me a king among the sons of Jesse, a law giver from the royal tribe of Judah. So David became the first covenanted king of Israel—God's visible church, or kingdom. Of Saul it is said: God gave him in his anger and took him away in his wrath. But David was *chosen of the Lord* to be a shepherd to, and a king over his people Israel. But let us have the covenant. I have made a covenant with my chosen, I have sworn unto David my servant, thy seed will I establish forever, and build up thy throne to all generations. I have laid help upon one that is mighty; I have exalted one chosen out of the people. I have found David my servant; with my holy oil have I anointed him; and I will beat down his foes before his face, and in my name shall his horn be axalted. He shall cry unto me, Thou art my father, my God, and the rock of my salvation. Also I will make him my first born, higher than the kings of the earth. My mercy will I keep for him forevermore, and my covenant shall stand fast with him. His seed also will I make to endure forever, and his throne as the days of heaven. My covenant will I not break, nor alter the thing that is gone out of my lips. Once have I sworn by my holiness that I will not lie unto David. His seed shall endure forever, and his throne as the sun before me. It shall be established forever as the moon, and as a faithful witness in heaven. This is *very strong*, and to me *very strange language*, if it does not teach that the visible kingdom over which David reigned, and the throne upon which David sat *are to endure forever.* The covenant says, *to all generations, as the days of heaven, as the moon, as the sun,* and *as a faithful witness in heaven.* I submit; does this not look very much like kingdom, or church *perpetuity?* And yet "our friends" would have us believe that God changed his mind, or lied unto David; for they tell us it was nothing but a Jewish Theocracy, has been abolished, annihilated, a "new church," the Christian kingdom, erected in its stead, while not a *vestage* of this kingdom of David is to be found in heaven or earth. But fortunately for us, God forestalled all such fanatical conclusions as these, when he said, My covenant I will not *break,* nor *alter* the thing that is gone out of my lips. Once have I sworn by my holiness that I will not *lie* unto David. His seed *shall endure forever* and *his throne as the sun before me.*

But listen to Isaiah on this point and see what perfect harmony exists between him and the Psalmist. For unto us a child is born, unto us a son is given; and the government shall be upon his shoulder; and his name shall be called Wonderful, Councellor, the Mighty God, the everlasting Father, the Prince of Peace. Of the increase of his government and peace there shall be no end, upon the throne of David and upon his kingdom, to order it, and to establish it with judgment and with justice from henceforth even forever. The zeal of the Lord of hosts will perform this. There it is; Christ, not upon the throne of a new church, or kingdom, *but upon the throne of David and upon his kingdom, to order and establish it forever and forever.* Here we find two converging lines that are to meet in perfect harmony in Christ—God's Son and David's son. The one line is governing the visible, and the other the invisible kingdom. These lines met at the birth of Christ; and the God-man mounted the throne of his father David, as its legitimate heir, on the day of Pentecost, and began to reign over the visible, as well as the spiritual kingdom; now a *dual* kingdom. And he will continue to reign until they become *one and the same identical kingdom,* in the end of time; and then the kingdom will be delivered up by the Son to God, even the Father, become the glorified kingdom, and *endure as the days of heaven; as the sun and as the moon forever, and as a faithful witness in heaven, to God's fidelity with his servant David.* This is what I call *church, or kingdom perpetuity.*

Now we will listen to the angel Gabriel and see how beautifully his testimony, on this point, blends and harmonizes with that of the prophet. And the angel said unto her, Fear not Mary; for thou hast found favor with God. And behold, thou shalt conceive in thy womb, and bring forth a son, and shalt call his name Jesus. He shall be great, and shall be called the Son of the Highest; and the Lord God shall give unto him the throne of his father David; and he shall reign over the house of Jacob forever; and of his kingdom there shall be no end. Now a gift implies the actual existence of three things. In fact there can be no gift without them. *A giver, a gift, and a receiver.* In this instance, the giver is *the Father,* the gift is *the throne of David,* and the receiver is *David's son and the Son of the Highest.* Therefore we conclude that the throne of David did *actually* exist at the ushering in of the Christian dispensation, that Christ did *actually* receive, and mount that throne, and that in connection with the Father's spiritual kingdom he will *actually* reign over the visible kingdom of his father David *forever*; and also that of this his dual kingdom *there shall actually be no end.* Does not this begin to look like *real* kingdom, or church *perpetuity sure enough ?*

But, in concluding this argument, we will give you the testimony of Peter, in behalf of all the apostles, on this point. Men and brethren, let me freely speak unto you of the patriarch David, that he is both dead and buried, and his sepulchre is with us unto this day. Therefore being a prophet, and knowing that God had sworn with an oath to him, that of the fruit of his loins, according to the flesh, he would raise up Christ to sit on his throne; he seeing this before, spake of the resurrection of Christ; that his soul was not left in hell, neither his flesh did see corruption. This Jesus hath God raised up, whereof we all are witnesses. It is *remarkably strange* that *all the apostles* would bear witness to the fact that God had raised Christ up from the dead, in fulfillment of his oath, to sit upon the throne and reign over the kingdom of David if that kingdom had already ceased to exist. The fact is we have found in these references, *a perfect chain of scriptural truth, harmonious throughout,* that forces us to the conclusion, that the visible kingdom under the Christian, is but the perpetuation of the same kingdom under the Jewish dispensation.

OUR THIRD ARGUMENT on church perpetuity is submitted in the form of questions, answered in the light of scripture.

First question. To whom was Jesus born a king? We will let Matthew answer first. Now when Jesus was born in Bethlehem of Judea in the days of Herod the king, behold, there came wise men from the east to Jerusalem, saying, Where is he that is born king of the Jews? for we have seen his star in the east, and are come to worship him. Now Luke may answer. And a superscription also was written over him in letters of Greek, and Latin, and Hebrew, THIS IS THE KING OF THE JEWS. Now John will answer. Then said the chief priests of the Jews to Pilate, Write not, The king of the Jews; but that he said, I am king of the Jews. Pilate answered, What I have written I have written. Or, in other words, What I have written is true and I will not change it. *He is king of the Jews.* He was born to be a king to the Jews, the rightful heir to the throne of his father David's kingdom. This is in keeping with God's oath of confirmation to David, and should be an end to all strife on this point.

Second question. Under what accusation was he crucified? We will go to John again for the answer. And Pilate wrote a title, and put it on the cross. And the writing was, JESUS OF NAZARETH THE KING OF THE JEWS. Born king of the Jews, and crucified king of the Jews.

Third question. When he became Governor, whom did he rule? Micah answers. But thou, Bethlehem Ephratah, though thou be little among the thousands of Juda, yet out of thee shall he come forth unto me that is to be ruler in Israel; whose goings forth have been from of old, from everlasting. Matthew confirms this testimony. And thou Bethlehem, in the land of Juda, art not the least among the princes of Juda: for out of thee shall come a Governor, that shall rule my people Israel. *Strange* if Christ was to be Governor and ruler of a "new church" that inspiration should make the sad mistake of placing him, under the Christian dispensation too, over the same visible kingdom that had outlived the old Jewish dispensation, and was destined, in connection with his spiritual kingdom, to outlive *time itself,* and ultimately become the kingdom of eternal glory.

Fourth question. Was Christ a king; and if so, over whom did he reign? Luke says when he made his triumphant entrance into Jerusalem that the whole multitude of disciples began to rejoice and praise God, saying, Blessed be the King that cometh in the name of the Lord; peace in heaven and glory in the highest. The Pharisees wanted him to rebuke his disciples for calling him a king; but Jesus answered if these should hold their peace the stones would immediately cry out. God says through Ezekiel, Behold I will take the children of Israel from among the heathen, and bring them unto their own land, and one king shall be king to them all; and they all shall have one shepherd; and my servant David (in the person of Christ), shall be their prince forever; and I will set my sanctuary in the midst of them forevermore. Yea I will be their God and they shall be my people; and the heathen shall know that I the Lord do sanctify Israel. Zechariah says, Rejoice greatly, O daughter of Zion; shout, O daughter of Jerusalem; behold, thy king cometh unto thee: he is just and having salvation. And Matthew points out the fulfillment of this prophecy in Christ. Tell ye the daughter of Zion, Behold thy king cometh unto thee. Pilate said to Jesus, Art thou the king of the Jews?

Jesus evaded the question, and said, My kingdom is not of this world: meaning the spiritual kingdom over which he then reigned, for he adds, but *now* is my kingdom not from hence. He had not yet assumed the reigns of the visible kingdom. But Pilate pressed the question, Art thou a king then? Jesus answered, Thou sayest that I am a king. To this end was I born, and for this cause came I into the world, that I might bear witness unto the truth—that I might bear faithful witness to the *covenanted truth of my Father God unto my father David,* mount his throne and perpetuate his kingdom through all time, and to all eternity.

Fifth question. To whom was Christ sent, and to whom did he send his twelve apostles? Christ said himself, I am not sent but unto the lost sheep of the house of Israel. Jesus also sent forth his twelve disciples, his subordinate officers, saying, Go not into the way of the Gentiles, and into any city of the Samaritans enter ye not: but go rather to the lost sheep of the house of Israel. And as ye go, preach, saying, The kingdom of heaven is at hand. And again he called his twelve disciples together, and gave them power and authority over all devils, and to cure diseases; and he sent them to preach the kingdom of God, and to heal the sick. The kingdom of heaven is at hand. The kingdom of God is preached. The visible kingdom—the tabernacle of David, is about to be set up again, under the new covenant, and united under Christ, the one king, with the spiritual kingdom. This union of the visible and spiritual kingdoms into one dual kingdom took place on the day of Pentecost. Joel says, Blow the trumpet in Zion, sanctify a fast, call a solemn assembly: gather the people, sanctify the congregation, assemble the elders, gather the children and those that suck the breasts: and then what Joel? let the bridegroom go forth of his chamber, and the bride out of her closet. Let Christ and the visible church meet as bride and groom *in holy spiritual wedlock* and I will pour out my Spirit upon all flesh; for in mount Zion and in Jerusalem shall be deliverance, and in the remnant whom the Lord shall call, then shall Jerusalem be holy; for the Lord dwelleth in Zion. And Peter said upon the day of Pentecost, This is that which was spoken by the prophet Joel; and it shall come to pass in the last days, saith God, I will pour out my Spirit upon all flesh: Christ mounted the throne of David then, on the day of Pentecost, and, as King of kings, will reign to the glory of God the Father, and to *the eternal perpetuation* of his dual kingdom. *This is church, or kingdom perpetuity.*

CHAPTER V.

THE ORDINANCES OF THE VISIBLE KINGDOM.

We will only notice three of these important ordinances; Preaching the Word, the Lord's Supper and Water Baptism.

PREACHING THE WORD.

Preaching, under the new, answers to prophecy, under the old dispensation. "It pleased God by the foolishness of preaching to save them that believe. For the preaching of the cross is to them that perish foolishness; but unto us which are saved it is the power of God." Our mission is to preach the *gospel* to every creature, to sow the seed of truth by all waters. Our field of labor is the world, and the seed we are commanded to sow is the word of God. *"Preach the word."* The word of God is quick and powerful. The word is *potent.* It has been tested; thrown in the crucible, but never found wanting. It always meets the emergency and fills the demand. The Celestial Empire, The Land of the Rising Sun, in brief, nearly the whole of the Oriental world, is wrapped in moral darkness and sepulchred in spiritual death. But the faithful preaching of the word, *in its potency*, will win all of these heathen nations, as an inheritance for Christ, and the uttermost parts of the earth as his rightful possession. We do well then if we preach *the gospel*, since so many preach almost everything else to the exclusion of the word. This word is the revealed will of God—the power of God unto salvation. And therefore infinitely better adapted to the wants of men, than Philosophy, Science, Mythology, or any thing else that we can possibly preach.

This word, which we preach, comes to all mankind with its lessons of salvation and promises of heaven. In it every man may find a sweet response to the yearnings of his own spirit; a chord of sympathy thrilling in unison with the deepest and loftiest experience of his own heart. It brings rest and strength to the soul amid all the conflicts of life. This blessed word describes all conditions of human life; and gives utterance to all the desires and emotions of the human soul. It has a song of triumph for the victor and a wail of defeat for the vanquished. It sparkles with the fervor and gladness of youth, celebrates the glory and strength of manhood; and bewails the sorrows and infirmities of old age. It exults in the mighty deeds of kings and conquerors, sympathizes with the poor and lowly, lifts up the fallen, delivers the oppressed and breathes the blessings of peace upon the quiet homes of domestic life. It describes with startling clearness the seductions of temptation, the conflicts of doubt and the miseries of skepticism. It searches the secret chambers of the heart, and brings to light its purest love and darkest hate; its highest joy and deepest grief. In other words, it compasses the utmost range of thought, feeling and desire; and sounds the utmost depth of motive, character and passion. It enters the lowliest home with the blessings of peace; kindles the light of hope in the darkest abode, and speaks in gentleness and kindness to the out cast and abandoned of earth. It nerves the weary arm with strength, inspires the heavy heart with hope and fills the longing soul with joy and gladness. It sets forth the most spiritual and heavenly truths in the lights and shadows of earthly scenes and human characters; and reveals to man the great fountain of justice, love and mercy, for all the world, in the person of Jesus. Then let us preach it, not as a fable, but as the inspired word of God—not in slavish fear or cowardly superstition, but in *loving humility* and *living faith,* and the world will acknowledge its efficiency in the yield of a hundred fold. For there is a naturalness of adaptation in the word to the wants of fallen humanity to be found no where else. Then away with your cold, philosophical reasoning, food it may be for the intellect, but famine to the soul, and let us have the gospel which sets forth the compassionate love of Jesus with a power that melts the hard and stony heart, long since invulnerable to the attacks of rhetoric and philosophy—the gospel that ravishes with its sweetness, and melts to deep contrition with its sympathy, the soul that could never be moved by flowery essays, or eloquent disertations. PREACH THE WORD.

THE LORD'S SUPPER.

There are just two *all-important* events in the system of human redemption, that were prefigured, or symbolized, under the old dispensation. These are respectively, *the death of Christ*, and *the conversion of the soul*. The death of Christ was symbolized by the Passover, and the conversion of the soul by the ordinance of Circumcision. But these grand events are still represented under the new dispensation. The regeneration of the soul is figured by the ordinance of Water Baptism; while the death of Christ is symbolized by the sacrament of the Lord's Supper.

God gave the ordinance of the Pass-over to Israel as a pledge that Christ would come and redeem the world. So when Jesus redeemed that pledge on the cross the Pass-over like a settled note became null and void. The Lord's table was erected in its room and stead, in the same church. For Jesus just after administering this ordinance to his apostles said, I appoint unto you a kingdom, as my Father hath appointed unto me, that ye may eat and drink at my table in my kingdom, and sit on thrones judging the twelve tribes of Israel. This sacred ordinance was instituted by the Saviour himself, on the same night in which he was betrayed. He had just eaten, with his disciples the last Pass-over, closing out the old dispensation, and foreshadowing, for the last time, the ushering in of the new, when he took the bread and wine, fit emblems of his broken body and shed blood, blessed, partook himself, and administered to his disciples; saying, as oft as ye eat this bread and drink this wine, ye do show the Lord's death till he come. This divine ordinance then, was to take the place of, and answer a similar purpose, under the new dispensation, to that of the Pass-over under the old.

The Pass-over had its origin in the fact, that, on the night before the departure of Israel from Egypt, the destroying angel passed over the houses of the Hebrews because of the blood of a lamb found on the door posts, while he slew the first born of all the Egyptians. This sacred festival was commemorative, and also typical in its nature. The great deliverance it commemorated was a striking type of the, still greater, salvation it foretold. Its chief design was to point out, through the sacrifice of its paschal lamb, the more important sacrificial offering of the Lamb of God. Christ identified himself with this paschal lamb, as its great antitype, when he substituted the Lord's Supper for the Pass-over, and on the same (Jewish) day became our Pass-over, sacrificed for us on the cross. The main purpose then, was accomplished at the death of Christ; and hence it was abrogated, as a part of the ceremonial law—abolished by Christ, as a part of the law of commandments contained in ordinances. It is gone; forever gone! And the Holy Eucharist, a simple but significant ordinance takes its place, and points the world with *index finger* back to Christ, just as its predecessor pointed forward to the Lamb of Hope yet to be slain.

The similarity of circumstances connected with these two ordinances bear me out in these assertions. Each of them marked a new era, or epoch, in the history of the church and the world. The sacrifice of the Pass-over was a lamb, evidently pointing, typically, to the Lamb slain for sin, the sacrificial death of which is celebrated in the Lord's Supper. Salvation was secured through the blood of each of these sacrifices; and not a bone of either was broken. The Jews ate the paschal lamb with bitter herbs; so christians eat the flesh and drink the blood of the Lamb of God, by faith, through the worm-wood and gaul of repentance and deep contrition of spirit. The children of Israel observed the feast of the Pass-over with their loins girded, and their feet shod, ready to take up the line of march for the promised land, and so the children of God partake of the sacrament of the Lord's Supper, acknowledging themselves, strangers and pilgrims on the earth, seeking a better country, that is an heavenly. The eucharistic Lamb was sacrificed on the same day of the week and year, on which the paschal lamb was slain; and the Pass-over, a mere shadow of good things to come, gave way to the substance, a purely spiritual ordinance, that points us to a new and living way into the holiest by the blood of Jesus.

But the controvercial point, in connection with this holy sacriment, has reference principle to the elements used. Are the bread and wine mere emblems, or the actual flesh and blood, of the slain Lamb? Christ said of the bread, This is my body, broken for you; and of the wine, This cup is the new testament in my blood. Did the Saviour really intend to teach, with reference to these elements, the mysterious, not to say absurd, doctrine of Transubstantiation; that the bread and wine are, in substance, verily changed into his literal flesh and blood? Did he not rather teach that they were emblematic of his broken body and shed blood; representing the hidden manna and the water of life, upon which the soul is expected to feast bountifully in the observance of this purely spiritual ordinance? It is just as unreasonable to claim that Jesus was speaking literally, and taught that the bread and wine were his real flesh and blood, as it would be to contend that because he said, This cup, that he meant the literal cup, not its contents, is the new testament in my blood.

But not only are these elements emblematic; this sacred ordinance itself is a beautiful symbol of the great communion of saints in heaven. Our Saviour doubtless alluded to this fact when he said, I will not drink henceforth of this fruit of the vine, *not blood*, until that day when I drink it new with you in my Father's kingdom. Just as the bread and wine are symbolical of the broken body and shed blood of Christ; so the entire ordinance is a striking type of a higher service, and a more glorious communion, around the sacramental table in heaven, where all the redeemed of earth shall sit down together and eat the marriage supper of the Lamb. Glorious communion indeed! The redeemed of every age and clime; the vast myriads of all nations, kindred, people and tongues, which stand before the throne and the Lamb; the hundred and forty and four thousand, seen by the Revelator; the General Assembly and church of the first born, and the vast multitudes which no man can number, clothed with white robes and bearing palms of victory in their hands; these will be the recognized communicants around this, *same perpetuated*, Sacramental Board in heaven, headed by the Great Master of Assemblies.

WATER BAPTISM.

Just when and where this holy ordinance was instituted no man can tell. Who was the administrator and the subject of the first instance of water baptism history does not reveal. Yet we have good and ample reasons for accepting it as a divine ordinance of no small import. The use of water in this sacred ordinance is no doubt owing to its qualities as the great element of purification: for "water and blood" were the divinely appointed symbols of moral renovation and atonement under the Mosaic Economy. This sacred ordinance is scripturally administered in the name of the Father, Son and Holy Ghost; and is, on the part of adults, a public profession of faith in Christ; and thus significant of regeneration, but by no means a regenerating ordinance.

The Bible recognizes a *spiritual*, as well as a *water* baptism; an *invisible*, as well as a *visible* baptism; a baptism *with the Holy Ghost*, as well as a baptism *with water*. And we do well to remember that of the two, the former is of *infinitely* more importance than the latter. The first, is the substance, the last the shadow: the water, *a mere emblem*, the spiritual, *a divine reality*: the one, simply an aswer of a good conscience, but the other, a washing of regeneration and a renewing of the soul by the Holy Ghost. Spiritual baptism is *salvation*; water baptism, but its figure. "The like *figure* where unto baptism doth now also save us." Temporal salvation in the ark was a figure of eternal salvation in heaven; and water was a visible sign, or line of distinction, between the saved and unsaved. Just so in these two baptisms, water, is the visible sign, or figure, of spiritual baptism, representing to the natural eye the line of distinction between the saved and the lost. With these *plain facts* before us, we are not so likely to *wrest* the Scriptures, and misapply passages referring to spiritual baptism, in order to prove *erroneous* views on the subject of water baptism. The connected circumstances must always decide as to which baptism reference is made, in the absence of direct, or positive proof. For instance, when the apostle says, one Lord, one faith, one baptism, the connection shows clearly that he had no reference whatever to water baptism. For there are lords many, faiths many and, in one sense, baptisms many. But there is only one Lord and Saviour, one *saving* faith and one baptism *essential to salvation.* "There is one body, and one Spirit, even as ye are called in one hope of your calling; one Lord, one faith, one baptism, one God and Father of all, who is above all, and through all, and in you all."

Good men, learned men, christian men have differed widely on this vexed question. Therefore we do not make water baptism *a test ordinance,* or unchristianize any whose views may not be in perfect harmony with ours. In *essentials* to salvation we insist on the closest possible unity of faith: in *non-essentials*, we grant the widest concievable liberty of thought; but in *all things* give us *unbounded charity.*

CHAPTER VI.

THE DESIGN OF WATER BAPTISM.

There are three distinct views held, as to the design of water baptism. For convenience we designate them as the Baptist, the Campbellite, and the Pedo-Baptist versions. Two out of these three, must of *necessity* be wrong, for water baptism can have but one *specific* design. In fact, all are agreed that but one of these versions *can be* true, that one of them *is* true. But which is true? This is the question to be settled.

THE BAPTIST VERSION says, water baptism is designed to symbolize the death, burial and resurrection of Christ. We join issue with this version, in the *first* place, because we find no authority for it in God's word. None of the passages relied upon by its advocates refer to water baptism at all. And if they did, unfortunately for them, they would prove just a little too much for their theory; and establish beyond all controversy the dogma of " baptismal regeneration."

We will now examine carefully two of their favorite, and most popular, passages on this version; and hope to be able to convince our readers that they have no reference to water baptism whatever, but refer solely to the baptism of the Holy Ghost. The first reads, Know ye not, that so many of us as were baptized into Jesus Christ were baptized into his death? Therefore we are buried with him by baptism into death: that like as Christ was raised up from the dead by the glory of the Father, even so we also should walk in newness of life. For if we have been planted together in the likeness of his death, we shall be also in the likeness of his resurrection. It does not require a critical eye to see that this passage refers only to spiritual baptism. Paul says, writing to persons all of whom had been baptized with water, Know ye not that *so many of us as were baptized into Jesus Christ, were baptized into his death.* Nothing could be plainer: all baptized with water; but only a part of them, with the Holy Ghost. But we are buried with Christ, by baptism into death. The context shows that this is a death unto sin. Then if it be water baptism, by which we are buried into this death, water baptism is essential to salvation, and the dogma of "baptismal regeneration" is established beyond the shadow of a doubt. There is but two horns to the dilemma, and our baptist friends must choose one or the other. It is either spiritual baptism, by which we are buried into death, or water baptism is essential to salvation. Which horn of the dilemma will you choose? Choose either and your version is gone, forever gone. Again the context teaches us, that this is a death unto sin which makes us alive unto God. It must therefore be a spiritual baptism; for water baptism has no power to kill unto sin, or to make alive unto God. Again the same agent that raised Christ from the dead enables us to walk in newness of life. That agent is the spirit by which the body of sin is destroyed and the soul freed from its condemning power.

> By water this could not have been;
> The burial was a death to sin.
> Not only *buried* the apostle said,
> But *planted, crucified* and *dead.*
> Thus we are buried into death
> By the Spirit the scripture saith.

The fact is the terms buried, planted, and crucified with him, are all figurative or metaphorical and denote the same thing—the death of the soul to sin, and its resurrection, through the baptism of the spirit, to newness of life. For ye are dead, *crucified,* and your life is hid, *buried, planted,* with Christ in God, through, spiritual baptism, the washing of regeneration and the renewing of the Holy Ghost. But Paul says we *are* buried: this is enough to show that it is not water baptism, for they were not under water at that time, yet they were buried even then. The idea that this is a burial in water, rather than into a death to sin, by which we are resurrected to newness of life, is as *soulless* as it is *senseless*. Paul says we are buried *into death*, not in water: And the Spirit alone has the power to kill, to sin and make alive to God, Hence the burial into death is by spiritual, and not by water, baptism. With Baptists, the burial is baptism, and baptism is the burial. But Paul says buried by baptism, making one the cause, the other the effect, one the agent and the other the action. He knew too much about rhetoric to say baptized by baptism, or buried by a burial. And yet this Baptist version, virtually charges him with just such nonsensical folly.

The second passage is very similar to the first. Buried with him by baptism, wherein also ye are risen with him through the faith of the operation of God, who hath raised him from the dead. This scripture explains itself. It shows that christians are buried with Christ in a baptism that has also resurrected them with him; so that they reckon themselves dead indeed unto sin, but alive unto God. It also teaches that this baptism is administered, in consequence of faith, upon our part, by the operation of God, who operates, in saving baptism, only through the agency of the Spirit; for by his Spirit we are baptized into Christ, says the Gospel. This burial is not baptism, but an effect of baptism. Cause and effect are different things but this version makes them the same thing, since one dip constitutes both the burial and the baptism.

To satisfy us that these sacred oracles are metaphorical, and refer only to spiritual baptism, with its natural results, we need but remember the following *truths*. A thing when literally planted must remain planted. A man literally crucified, is actually put to death on a cross. In a person literally dead, life must be extinct. To be literally buried, we must remain in that into which we are buried. And to be buried into death, is not simply to be dipped, or plunged into water, and taken out immediately. For we remain dead and our lives remain hid, or buried, with Christ in God. We *are* buried with him by baptism into death. And it is just as unreasonable to contend that we can not be buried by baptism into death spiritually, without being actually immersed in water, as it would be to claim that we can not be crucified spiritually, unless we be literally put to death on a cross, or that we can not have spiritual life, unless we actually eat the literal flesh and drink the literal blood of Christ. What an absurdity!

We join issue with this version in the *second* place because it makes water baptism and the Lord's Supper represent one and the same thing. If true, this is passing strange indeed, since the great event signified only by the Passover, when seen through the dim light of prophecy, must now be represented by two sacred ordinances, though a historic fact hoary with the weight of centuries; while the conversion of the soul, an event that fills the courts of heaven with joy and gladness, once symbolized by the ordinance of Circumcision, though now occupying a more prominent place, should yet be entirely overlooked, in the institution of ordinances, under the Gospel dispensation. We can not believe it. Now, if this version be true, water baptism is a *sign* of the death, burial and resurrection of Christ; but Jesus said himself that no such sign should be given that wicked generation, but the sign of the prophet Jonas; "For as Jonas was three days and three nights in the whale's belly, so shall the son of man be three days and three nights in the heart of the earth." Here is another dilemma; Christ *versus* the Baptist version. Where think you we will be most likely to find the truth; in this version or in the words of Jesus?

We object to this version, in the third place, because, if it be true, water baptism has never filled its mission in the world. For no mode or manner of baptism ever practiced by the advocates of this version even faintly represents the death, burial and resurrection of Christ, or any one of them. Even trine immersion will not fill the bill. Compare immersion with a burial and you will find nothing to warrant the assumption that the one symbolizes the other. Dipping has not the slightest resemblance to the mode of burying people in any part of the world. Who ever dreamed of seeing a subject for the tomb wade in the grave knee deep and then be plunged into the sod by another person? Who ever heard of a people that buried the living in order to secure their death? Who ever saw a man buried one moment and resurrected the next? Where is the resemblance? It can not be found for the simple reason that it is not there to find. And yet strange to say, the advocates of this scriptureless version, let them dip once or thrice, take their subjects out of the water as soon as possible and vainly imagine they have represented the agonizing death, three days burial and the triumphant resurrection of Christ. But

"Water baptism was not designed
To set before a person's mind,

THE CAMPBELLITE VERSION. 67

<blockquote>
A <i>grave</i>—a <i>funeral</i>, and <i>polution</i>,
But rather does it show ablution—
A cleansing by the Saviour's blood,
With that baptism performed by God:
Water baptism no doubt is meant,
This work of God to represent."
</blockquote>

THE CAMPBELLITE VERSION claims that the design of water baptism is to secure the remission of sins. We object to this version, *first*, because it stands in positive contradiction to God's Word. We simply give a part of the scriptures that this version contradicts without note, or comment, as neither is necessary. He that believeth on him is not condemned: but he that believeth not is condemned already, because he hath not believed in the name of the only begotten Son of God. He that believeth on the Son hath everlasting life, and he that believeth not the Son shall not see life. To him give all the prophets witness, that through his name whosoever believeth in him shall receive remission of sins.

<blockquote>
Then in order to secure
  The remission of our sins,
We need not seek a pond impure
  And plunge our bodies in:
For, if we but in Christ believe,
  We'll meet the <i>Lord's</i> condition,
Baptism, <i>spiritual</i>, receive,
And with it <i>full</i> remission.
</blockquote>

We differ with this version, in the *second*

place, because God saved persons under the old dispensation, without water baptism; and we believe he still saves in the same way under the new dispensation. He is the same God, in every respect, that he always was—the same yesterday, to-day and forever—in whom there is no variableness, neither shadow of turning. The relation we sustain to God, as sinners, is also exactly the same under both dispensations. The Bible no where intimates that God has made the slightest change, either as to the means, or condition of salvation. If we learn the means by which, and the condition upon which God saved men at any period in the world's history, we have them then for all time, past and future. Paul says, By grace are ye saved through faith; and that (*salvation*) not of yourself; it is the gift of God: not of works lest any man should boast. Here we find faith, with what faith implies, *the condition* of salvation. But again he says, Not by works of righteousness which we have done (hence not by *water baptism*), but according to his mercy, he saved us, by the washing of regeneration, and the renewing of the Holy Ghost. Here we find the *instrument* or *agent* through which we obtain remission of sins—the Holy Ghost. Once more: Paul says, Without the shedding of blood there is no remission. Here we find the *means,* which must be applied in order to the remission of sins—the blood of Christ. We learn then, from these passages of scripture, that grace is the *provisional,* faith the *conditional,* God the *original,* Christ the *procuring,* or *meritorious,* and the Holy Spirit the *instrumental* cause of our salvation. And when these causes *all* unite, no matter whether water baptism has been administered or not, the effect *is* produced, we have *remission of sins,* and our souls are saved for time and eternity.

We take issue with this version, in the *third* place because, the scriptures teach that *spiritual baptism* is essential to the remission of sins. Paul says, We being many are one body in Christ. For as many of you as have been baptized into Christ have put on Christ. For by one Spirit are we all baptized into one body and have been all made to drink into one Spirit.

> "The Spirit's baptism saves from sin,
> And to Christ's body brings us in:
> Of this one body, Christ is head,
> If not the body must be dead.
> The *water* this may *represent,*
> But we should never be content
> To experience but the outward sign,
> And live without the work divine."

We find fault with this version, in the *fourth* place, because it is not in harmony with the answer of Paul and Silas to the Jailer's question, Sirs what must I do to be saved? Believe on the Lord Jesus Christ and thou shalt be saved, and thy house. Here is proffered salvation, through faith, without water baptism, either *implied* or *expressed*.

> "No treasure can we have above,
> Without that faith which works by love.
> In ancient times there were not a few,
> That might be called an outward Jew:
> While with real Jews they had no part,
> Not being circumcised in heart.
> In modern times there are many too
> No better than the ancient Jew:
> With water they have been baptized,
> But never have they realized
> The Spirit's baptism on the heart;
> Therefore with Christ they have no part."

We differ with this version, in the *fifth* place, because Paul said to the Corinthians, I thank God that I baptized none of you, but Crispus and Gaius: and I baptized also the household of Stephanas; besides, I know not whether I baptized any other. For Christ sent me not to baptize, but to preach the Gospel. Strange indeed, if water baptism be designed to secure the remission of sin—*essential to salvation*—that Paul, with all his zeal for Christ, should thank God that he had been instrumental in saving so few. I am sure no Campbellite minister would be guilty of using such language, with reference to immersion. For,

"They often make this false assertion,
"*No one is saved without immersion!*"
That God has neither son or daughter,
But such as have been under water.
God has no way that he can save,
But only through a watery grave;
"Ho! every mother's son and daughter;
Here's the Gospel in the water!"
They say there is but one condition,
On which we can obtain remission;
Under the water we must go,
For Alexander tells us so!
The Bibles that he wrote they read;
And these form their religious creed.
If we all through *his version* look,
We'll find no *baptism* in his Book.
He says *immersion*, and not *baptism;*
This *surely* then, is *Campbellism!*"

We object to this version, in the *sixth* place, because the scriptures relied upon, by its advocates, do not sustain it. We will examine a few of their favorite passages on the design of water baptism.

FIRST PASSAGE: Then Peter said unto them, repent, and be baptized every one of you in the name of Jesus Christ for the remission of sins, and ye shall receive the gift of the Holy Ghost. Peter was not discussing the *efficacy of water baptism*. He was pricking the hearts of the Jews who believed in the Father and the Holy Ghost, but rejected Christ. Their *great sin* was the crucifixion of the Messiah. The *burden* of Peter's sermon to them was, *sal-*

vation only through this rejected, crucified Saviour. The leading thought in the passage is a repentance and a baptism, which recognize Christ as the Son of God and the Saviour of the world.

THIRD PASSAGE: Go ye into all the world, and preach the Gospel to every creature. He that believeth and is baptized shall be saved; but he that believeth not shall be damned. In this commission we have the essentials to salvation; faith and spiritual baptism. But were the Scriptures silent on this subject, common sense ought to teach us to predicate salvation to *spiritual*, rather than water baptism.

FOURTH PASSAGE: Except a man be born of water and of the Spirit, he can not enter into the kingdom of God. The exegesis is simply this: Jesus was talking to Nicodemus; he introduced the subject of the new birth. Nicodemus thought he had reference to a second natural birth. Christ explained by referring to the natural as a *water* birth; a reference common among the Jews; and to the Supernatural as a *Spiritual* birth. Man is *first*, as all physicians know, born of, or through the agency of water, and can not be born without it. His is *a water birth, or a birth by water*. But man is *next*, as Christ declares, born of, or through the agency of the

THE SPIRITUAL BIRTH.

Spirit. He can not be born without it. His is *most emphatically a spiritual birth, or a birth by the Spirit.* In plain English Christ said, Except this *spiritual,* follow the natural birth a man cannot enter the kingdom of God. That which is born of the flesh is flesh; and that which is born of the Spirit is spirit. Marvel not that I said unto thee, Ye must be born again.

" 'Tis water baptism; some will say,
And tell us there's no other way
We can become a child of God,
And feel the virtue of Christ's blood.
They boldly make this false assertion,
There is no birth but by immersion.
They'll own no person as a brother,
Unless he does revere their mother.
Be this a river, lake or pond,
Of her they seem extremely fond;
They think her worthy of all honor,
And place their love so much upon her,
That whether they do speak or write,
She's in their thoughts both day and night.
And now I ask do they not rather
Give her more honor than their father.
'Tis the strangest notion yet on earth,
That '*water baptism is a birth;*'
Unless they do embrace that other,
That *literal water* is their *mother;*
Then who's their father? For surely he,
Must married to their mother be;
This truth the Scriptures do decide,
The church is God's own lawful bride;
He'll never own a son or daughter,
Whose mother is a pond of water."

SYMBOLIZES SPIRITUAL BAPTISM.

THE PEDO-BAPTIST version contends that water baptism is designed to symbolize spiritual baptism; that it is a *visible* sign of an *invisible* work; a divine ordinance, in the reception of which its subjects publicly profess faith in Christ; either by their own, or the *guardian* act of their parents. With this version our faith is in perfect harmony. And since we have shown both of the others to be false, this version must of *necessity* be true. In proving them false we have *negatively* proven this to be true. But Peter *positively* declares that water baptism is not the putting away of the filth of the flesh, but the answer of a good conscience toward God. Then the baptism, *essential* to salvation, is that of the *Spirit*, while water baptism is but its beautiful and appropriate symbol.

"Yet many think it very brave,
To talk about a *watery grave!*
Yet stranger still, some others do,
Make it a *birth*, and *burial* too.
'*Baptism a funeral and a birth!*'
Was e'er a thing so strange on earth?
That we must under water go,
A burial and a birth to show."
When by one Spirit we're baptized,
Then is Christ's blood to us applied;
Then does the life of faith begin,
We live to Christ, but die to sin:
Our life with Christ, in God is hid,
And here's the baptism we all need.

CHAPTER VII.

The Mode of Water Baptism.

Water baptism does not consist in mode or form. By mode we simply mean the way, or manner, in which water baptism should be administered. All are agreed that the mode adopted should be *scriptual* that the way we administer this sacred ordinance should have the sanction of divine authority. But the Christian world is not agreed as to what is the scriptural mode of water baptism. Some claim that *immersion*, and others that *affusion*, is the mode taught in the Scriptures. Of the two, we *conscientiously* believe, affusion is the apostolic, and *only scriptural*, mode of administering water baptism. And if the *validity* of water baptism depends upon conformity to the apostolic manner of administration, we do not hesitate one moment to pronounce immersion *invalid*, as well as *unscriptural*. But to the law and the gospel for the settlement of this question; *for the Bible must be our guide.*

"To this fair proposition no one will object,
Who really believes his creed is correct.
Then too them we will go and find what they say,
Than this, I am certain, their's no better way."

Immersion is not a Scriptural Mode of Water Baptism.

First Argument. Webster says in defining this ordinance, "it is the application of water to a person, as a religious ceremony." But immersion is an application of a subject to water, and not of water to a subject. Therefore, according to acknowledged authority, immersion is not water baptism.

Second Argument. There is no uniformity of opinion, or practice, among immersionists. It is optional with them whether they choose a river, lake, pond or trough; water two or five feet deep. The candidate may immerse any where from one-fourth to nine-tenths of his own body and the administrator the remainder. Some dip but once, others thrice; some backwards, others forwards; some about one-half, and others nothing but the head of the subject.

> "Some plunge them three times, and others but once,
> And each thinks the other is acting the dunce:
> While those that stand off and look at the fight,
> Conclude that in this, they are both of them right.
> If dipping is baptism, to me it seems droll,
> That dipping one-half. is baptizing the whole.
> Yet if dipping is baptism, then must all men see,
> That the part dipped by each, a baptism must be!
> If each dips but half, no intelligent soul,
> Can think this is equal to dipping the whole.

When the work of immersing is thus done by two,
There's one-half with which each had nothing to do!
Here's a poser, for those who make the assertion,
That "immersion is baptism, and baptism immersion."

THIRD ARGUMENT. Immersionists make an egregious blunder, in claiming that the Greek word *bap-ti-zo,* of which *bap-to* is the root, and *bap-ti-zo, bap-tis-ma,* &c., are derivatives, is *specific;* and hence points out the way, manner, or mode, of administering water baptism. While, the fact is *bap-ti-zo* is *generic,* and consequently does not express mode at all. It simply tells us *what* to do; but not *how* to do it. It says *baptize,* but, is as *silent as death,* on the *mode* of baptizing. To sustain their position, on this point, immersionists must prove that *bap-ti-zo* means to dip; *only* to dip, and *always* to dip. But when they go to the Greek lexicons they fail to find that *bap-ti-zo* signifies to dip; *only* to dip, and *always* to dip. For Mr. Carson says, "I have all the Lexicographers and Commentators against me in this opinion." So with the classic writers, the Greek and Latin fathers and the numerous translations into other languages, as well as our own version; they are *all* against this position. And yet,

That it must be by *dipping,* some people declare:
But we've read the Bible through and *know* its not there.
For many long years, some immersers have been

Laboring to prove that "*baptize* means *put in*,"
And others, not knowing what they're about
Are trying to prove that it means " to take out."
Immersion puts in, and *emersion takes out,*
But that baptize means either, I very much doubt.
Then no one should make the reckless assertion,
That water baptism, *in mode*, is immersion.

FOURTH ARGUMENT. There can not be *one instance* of water baptism cited, in the Bible, in which immersion was *evidently* the mode of administration. The only possible way to get a case of *dipping* is by inference. For the word *immersion* is not to be found in the Bible. Neither is *dip, plunge, submerge, or souze*, in connection with the administration of the ordinance of water baptism.

"Take the Scriptures my brother, and read them all thro',
And you doubtless will find what I've said to be true ;
If not, mark the places, each chapter and verse,
Where proof is direct, that baptize means immerse :
If such proof is not found, don't dispute the assertion,
That except for *destruction*, there was no immersion."

FIFTH ARGUMENT. There are instances of water baptism on record, in which immersion was impossible.

First instance. Paul had been three days in Damascus, without eating, or drinking, in deep penitence and prayer. The Lord sent Ananias to the house of Judas where he found Paul, and said, Brother Saul, the Lord, *even* Jesus, that appeared to thee in the way as thou camest, hath sent me that thou mightest receive thy sight, and be filled with the Holy Ghost. And immediately there fell from his eyes as it had been scales; and he received sight forthwith, and arose, and was baptized. Paul was not immersed in the house of Judas, where he arose and was baptized. And he who believes that he went off to some river, and was immersed, can believe anything he pleases, *proof*, or *no proof*. The fact is, there is not a single instance on record, in which the apostles took subjects to river, pond, or lake for the purpose of baptizing them. And in this instance, Ananias, knowing Paul had received the Spirit, said, *Arise* and be baptized; and he *arose* and *was baptized*. Immersion, in this instance, was an impossibility; therefore it is not *a scriptural mode* of water baptism.

"Well may the reader be surprised
When folks lie down to be baptized,
As every Bible reader knows,
That for baptism, Paul arose,"
And not a man on earth can prove,
That he, for baptism, one step did move!

Second instance. Paul and Silas had been cast into prison, then thrust into the inner prison, and their feet made fast in the stocks. At midnight they prayed and sang praises unto God, a great earthquake shook the foundations of the prison of Phillippi, the doors flew open, the bands of the prisoners were all loosed and the keeper was about to kill himself, supposing they had all escaped, when Paul said, Do thyself no harm: for we are all here. The jailer sprang in, fell trembling before Paul and Silas, brought them out of the inner prison and said, Sirs, what must I do to be saved? They answered, Believe on the Lord Jesus Christ, and thou shalt be saved and thy house. So the jailer took them the same hour of the night, washed their stripes, and was baptized, he and all his, straightway; that is, *immediately*, even before they left the outer prison; for they refused to go out privily, but demanded that the magistrates take them out openly. A strange place for immersion, in a heathen jail. *Impossible!* But,

> "Some think they did the jailer take,
> Out to some river, pond, or lake:
> That they most surely took him off,
> Water to find; or made a trough,
> Or had a pool to dip him in;
> Many such guesses there have been,
> And all are subject to a lecture,
> Who disbelieve what they *conjecture*."
> We learn they made no delay,
> But baptized him and his *straightway*.
> No truth then, in the base assertion,
> That the jailer's baptism was by immersion.

Third instance. The baptism of the three thousand, on the day of Pentecost, could not

THE DAY OF PENTECOST.

have been by immersion. If the apostles devoted five hours to baptizing, they must have baptized one every six seconds. Who can believe they immersed that rapidly? Or who, without the slightest intimation, not to say *proof*, can believe that they immersed at all? It is *unreasonable*, not to say *absurd*, to claim such a thing.

Against stern facts to argue, confusion surely brings;
To facts we always must submit, for they are stubborn things.
If tnat can be that can not be, let some one tell us how:
For facts and figures never before *mere conjectures* bow,
Then show not your ignorance, in the groundless assertion,
That "on the day of Pentecost, baptism was by immersion."

SIXTH ARGUMENT. Bible immersions are not water baptisms. The Bible records no immersion of men, except for their destruction. Instance, those who did not enter Noah's Ark, the hosts of Pharaoh at the Red Sea, and the immersion of Jonah for his disobedience: also a *swine immersion*, because possessed by a legion of devils. All of these subjects perished except Jonah, who through prayer, was saved *from immersion*. We believe these are all the instances of immersion that Inspiration saw fit to record; therefore we conclude that Bible immersion, at least, is not *a scriptural mode* of water baptism.

From the teachings of Scripture we draw this deduction,
That there was no *immersion*, except for *destruction!*
Now this is *the truth*, and we further remark,
Those were saved *from immersion*, who entered the Ark.
That 'twas a figure of baptism, can not be ignored,
As over the Ark the water was poured;
And it can't be denied that those were accursed,
Who for their *unbelief*, were *truly immersed!*
Then again: Bible readers must all be apprised,
That the children of Israel were *truly baptized.*
From Moses we have this plain declaration,
That their foes were *immersed* upon that occasion:
All those who were *plunged*, were surely accursed;
While of the subjects of *baptism, not one was immersed!*
Of all those baptized, not one was plunged in;
And all those immersed, were *immersed for their sin.*
When back-slidden Jonah was over-board thrown,
The *plunging* he got, was "*immersion alone.*"
Perhaps some immersers, will say in this case
"That while under water, conversion took place,
And that here is good proof, that a three days *immersion*
Of the subject, effected a *real* conversion."
To such, we would say, we think it more fair,
To attribute all this to effectual prayer!
From all these plain facts, we draw this deduction.
That 'twas not for *salvation*, but for their *destruction.*
So we think we may *truthfully* make this assertion,
That except for *destruction*, there was no *immersion.*

SEVENTH ARGUMENT. The passages, and instances relied upon by its advocates, do not prove immersion to be a scriptural mode of water baptism. The passages referred to, we have already noticed, under the head of design, and shown them to be references to *spiritual*, and not to water baptism.

PHILIP AND THE EUNUCH. 83

We first instance, the baptism of the Eunuch. Philip and the Eunuch both went down (*eis*) to, or into, the water and Philip baptized him. They both came up (*ek*) from, or out of, the water. The original, or a correct translation, you see, gives no countenance to the idea of immersion. But we will critically examine the translation in our own version, and see if it contains any proof of immersion. Philip and the Eunuch *both went* down into, and *both came* up out of the water. There is no proof here that one *put* the other in, or *took* him out. For if *into* means under, they both *went* under; and if *out of* means from under, they both *came* from under. Hence, if these prepositions prove that *one* was immersed, they *necessarily* prove that *both* were immersed. Again, if they do not prove the immersion of *both,* they can not prove the immersion of *either*. But how can they prove the immersion of *either,* or *both,* when they can not, even, prove the water to have been ankle deep. The matter stands thus: if *either*, then *both* were immersed; but only *one* was baptized: therefore immersion is not *a scriptural mode* of water baptism.

" Did Philip put the Eunuch in?
Is the question, and long has been:
Of this the Scriptures do not speak,
Neither the English nor the Greek.
But in the context *both* agree,

> That *sprinkled* the nations all should be,
> And Philip ne'er made such a blunder,
> As to think that *sprinkle* meant *put under.*
> So the record tells all the rest;
> He granted the Eunuch his request:
> And when baptized, as the Scriptures say,
> He went *rejoicing* on his way:
> But had he been baptised by dipping,
> He *doubtless* would have gone off dripping."

We next instance, baptism by John the Baptist. The fact that John was called, "the Baptist," does not prove that he was an immersionist. For if so, it would prove that he was the *only immersionist,* being the only one called a Baptist. John baptized in Enon, near to Salim, because there was much water, or many waters there. We cannot tell whether the "much water" was at Enon, or Salim. But admit that it was at Enon, and this does not prove that it was necessary to, or used for, the purpose of immersing the thousands of people who came to John's baptism, and needed much water for other purposes. But admit that the "much water," in this case, strengthens the immersion theory; and you are *forced* to concede, that, in every other case of baptismal record, the want of "much water" weakens the argument in favor of immersion.

John was a Local Preacher, each Bible reader knows:
He went not to the people, as the traveling preacher goes.
But the people of Judea, and of Jerusalem,

Came to hear him preach, and he taught and baptized them.
When such multitudes assembled, much water they would need,
But unless the multitudes were great, of *much* we do not read.
Much he would need for many folks, if he did not baptize any;
If he immersed, 'twould take as much to baptize few as many.
I'm very sure that in John's day, there was no dipping done,
Because the law required none, it might be done in fun.
So then, we rightfully conclude, that this is man's invention,
Since *immersing, plunging, dipping in,* the Scriptures no where mention.

John also baptized (*en*) at, or in, Jordan. If *in,* this, however, does not even prove that he went into the water ankle deep, if at all; much less does it prove that he *immersed* the people that he baptized. To get a case of immersion, even in this instance, the advocates of this theory must first *assume* that they were in the water; they must then *conjecture* that the water was deep enough for dipping; and then *guess*, after all, that John *plunged them in,* they know not *why, how,* or *how often.* With all of these facts before us we are *thoroughly* convinced that *immersion is not a scriptural mode* of water baptism.

Yet, many seem to think that they must preach and write,

And "compass *sea* and *land* to make a *proselyte*."
They say that *they're* commissioned to teach the people how
The saints of old were baptized, and *how to do it now;*
They tell us 'twas by *dipping;* and make the bold assertion,
"*There is no Gospel baptism, where there's no immersion.*"
Determined all shall see, that baptism is immersion,
The Scriptures they've perverted, to an *immersion version!*
If you will take this version, and with care all through it look,
You'll find they've driven baptism entirely from the Book.
Baptism is not in it; but the *Latin word* immersion,
Which has *no religious meaning.* Oh, what a gross perversion!
Being *under* is *immersion*, whatever is the cause;
But 'tis not *water baptism*, so called by *Christian* laws.
To *immerse* is to *put under;* of this there is no doubt:
This is its *only* meaning; then, it never means *take out.*
So, if nothing but immersion, by Jesus was intended;
When you get them *under water,* the work if fully ended:
For surely no one dare make such a false assertion,
As to say, that *taking out* belongs to the word *immersion;*
It only means *put in;* why then should you do more?
For taking of them *out, undoes* what you *did* before.
Why, then, I ask, do more than just to put them *under?*
"What God together joins, let no man put assunder;"
Nor should we join together, what God has disunited:
And who so doeth this, for *crime* should be indicted.
Yet this they surely do, who make this false assertion,
That "*immersion is baptism;* and *baptism is immersion!*"

AFFUSION IS A SCRIPTURAL MODE OF WATER BAPTISM.

PROOF FIRST. Water baptism, as we have

shown, symbolizes spiritual baptism, and therefore should be administered in the same way. The New Testament has but little to say on the *mode* of baptism, the Old Testament having already settled this matter. "Thus shalt thou do unto them to cleanse them, sprinkle water of purifying upon them." Again, "So shall he (Christ) sprinkle many nations." But no prophet of God ever said that any of his people should be dipped, plunged, or immersed, either in water or spirit. They speak of *sprinkling* water, and *giving* the Spirit, *pouring* water, and the Spirit, baptizing *with* water, and *with* the Holy Ghost. Spiritual baptism is by *affusion*. Peter, in speaking of spiritual baptism, said, "poured out," "shed forth," and "fell on them." God says, by the mouth of Joel, I will pour out my Spirit upon all flesh. Peter said, on the day of Pentecost, this is that which was spoken by the prophet Joel. And it shall come to pass in the last days, saith God, I will pour out my Spirit upon all flesh. But John the Baptist said of Christ, he shall baptize you with the Holy Ghost and *with* fire. Here is *a clear case* of spiritual baptism by affusion. Then water baptism, fitly to represent the baptism of the Spirit, must be administered, either by sprinkling or pouring; for the Spirit comes down like dew, descends like rain, is poured out, shed forth, or falls on its subjects. This is in perfect harmony with the prophecy of Ezekiel: "Then will I sprinkle clear water upon you, and ye shall be (ceremonially) clean, from all your filthiness and from all your idols will I cleanse you."

> From these plain scriptures, we reach this conclusion,
> That *water baptism must be by affusion;*
> For they show there's *no truth,* in the assertion,
> That, God for his people ordained an immersion.
> They also rivet, upon our attention
> This fact, *immersion* is of man's invention.
> We are *forced* then, to the *lawful* conclusion,
> That *scriptural baptisms, are all by affusion.*

PROOF SECOND. There are *instances* in which water baptism was *evidently* administered by affusion. The baptism of Cornelius, and his house, must have been by affusion. They received the Holy Ghost, and it reminded Peter of John's baptism *with* water, because "it fell on them, purifying their hearts by faith." Then Peter said, Can any man forbid water, that these should not be baptized, which have received the Holy Ghost as well as we. So they were baptized, *then* and *there,* in the name of the Lord, by *affusion. Christ's baptism was of necessity by affusion.* He was a Priest, "a minister of the circumcison" lived under and fulfilled *every jot and tittle of the law* which required sprinkling. When he came and demanded baptism of John, it was that the *law* might be fulfilled, and he *consecrated,* at the appointed age, to the priestly office. And when the Scribes and Pharisees demanded his authority for ministering the priestly office at the Temple, he pointed them to John's baptism, saying, is it from heaven, or of men? As much as to say, here is my authority; here I was anointed above my fellows. The priests, at their consecration, were anointed with oil, after the water had been sprinkled upon them; but Christ, with the Holy Spirit, without measure, at his baptismal consecration to the office that made him "a Priest forever after the order of Melchisedec." True Jesus came *to,* and was doubtless baptized *in* Jordan; but this does not prove that he was *even in* the water, much less does it prove that he was under the water, though the original says he came up *from* the water. The translators of our version played upon the prepositions in this case, as in others, to try to make it read like it was dip. They were "*Pedo-immersionists,*" but dared not translate it dip, plunge, or immerse? But immersionists ask, why John baptized in Jordan, if he did not immerse? We answer, because he chose to do so. It was a convenient place for the multitudes to assemble. They could get plenty of water there. We ask, why did John baptize, in the wilderness, in Bethabara, and where Christ abode, if he did not sprinkle or pour? *No answer.* Did John baptize on dry land, and consequently by affusion? Or did Christ live *in the water?* Of course, Christ did not abide in the water; then John baptized by affusion.

Some think Christ was plunged, without any doubt,
Because, of *the water,* he was said to *come out.*
It is "*apo,*" from. From the water he came;
Carson and Conant acknowledge the same.
" He came from the water;" So says the New Version,
Translated by those who believe in immerson!
These immersionists say " Christ did not come out,"
Because "*apo* means *from,*" without any doubt.
If he did not *come out,* how could he *go in?*
Or how could his baptism, a *dipping* have been?
The baptism of Christ, and of sinners we see,
Were not *just* alike, such a thing could not be.
John taught his subjects, that they must need repent,
The baptism of Christ, could have no such intent.
Their baptism referred to remission of sin,
Regarding the Saviour, this could not have been.
But now let me say, under that dispensation,
Thirty was the age, for the Priest's consecration.
And none can tell why his age they should mention,
Unless his baptism was for this intention.
The law said *sprinkle,* therefore the conclusion
Jesus was *baptized,* and that by *affusion.*

All Israel was baptized at the Red Sea by affusion. Paul said, All our fathers were under the cloud, and all passed through the sea; and were all baptized unto Moses in the cloud and in the sea; and all did drink of that Spiritual

Rock that followed them; and that Rock was Christ. Christ was present then at this baptism. He administered the ordinance. Perhaps these were the first subjects, and Christ the first administrator of this sacred ordinance. But *how* did Christ baptize them? Not by immersion, for they passed over *dry shod*. Then it must have been by affusion, for the Psalmist says "The clouds poured out water" upon them, as God led his people, by the hand of Moses, through his path in the great waters and his way in the sea. This is a *clear* case of water baptism by *affusion*. Therefore affusion is a *scriptural* mode of water baptism.

> To be sure *Bible readers* must all be apprized,
> That the children of Israel were *truly baptized;*
> How this *could be dipping*, no one has yet found,
> For they passed through the sea upon the dry ground!
> We've a word now to say about Dr. Carson,
> That logical, bold, and renowned *Baptist* Parson
> Who speaking of Moses, says, as we may read,
> "*He got a dry dip.*" A dry dip indeed!
> This is the best dip I've read about yet,
> But the dip Pharaoh got, was really wet.
> He may choose the *wet dip*, I am certain that I,
> If I must have *a dip*, would prefer one that's dry!
> Once more we're forced to the *happy* conclusion,
> That water baptism *must be* by *affusion*.

PROOF THIRD. Many of the *places,* where water baptism was administered, prove that it was by affusion. Neither John, nor any of the apostles ever left house, city, or village, to baptize any one. Wherever they preached, the record shows, that *then* and *there* they also baptized. With immersionists the *place,* in one or two instances, has a *great deal* to do with the mode; but in all other instances they *hoot* at the idea that the place of administration should have any thing *at all* to do with the manner of baptism. They should remember that John not only baptized in Jordan and Enon; but *also* in Bethabara, beyond Jordan and where Christ abode: and that the twelve and seventy went into cities and villages where they "made and baptized more disciples than John" ever did in Jordan, or elsewhere. As to place, there are many instances of baptismal record where it *could not* have been by immersion; none where it is *unquestionably certain* that it could have been by immersion: none where it could not have been by affusion; and many where it *must of necessity* have been by affusion. Therefore we affirm that the *places* of water baptism prove *affusion to be the scriptural mode.*

This proof against immersion, in scripture we have found,
That many hundred thousand men were baptized on dry ground.
To call this baptism, *dipping*, is what we can not see!
For baptism on dry land, a dipping *could not* be.
This *death-blow* to immersion, against their creed must stand,

Till they immerse some one or more, *while standing on dry land.*
Then turn the subject as we may, up comes the *right* conclusion:
Water baptism, as to mode, is always by affusion.

PROOF FOURTH. The Scriptures always say baptized *with* water, but never *in* water. In, is used five times, in connection with baptism, but simply points out the place—tells where the baptism occured. While *with*, is used seventeen times, nine referring to water, and eight to spiritual baptism, *always* points to the element used, and indicates *clearly* the mode of administration. What John did *with* water he called baptism; and what Christ did *with* Spirit he called baptism. That one was by affusion we know; that the other was not by affusion, no man can prove. That neither was by immersion, is a self-evident fact. Because we *can not* dip a subject *with* an element; but *in* an element. If we dip at all it must be *in*, and not *with* water. Here is the scripture; sprinkle water, give the Spirit; pour water, pour the Spirit; baptize *with* water, and baptize *with* the Holy Ghost.

Christ and John baptized *with*, so the Scriptures say
'Twas *pouring out* and *falling on,* the only *scriptural* way.
That 'tis a better way there's no shadow of doubt,
Than *plunging people in* and *pulling of them out.*
Once more are we *driven,* to the *happiest conclusion,*
That both of these baptisms were administered by affusion.

CHAPTER VIII.

The Subjects of Water Baptism.

With reference to the subjects of water baptism, the Christian world is divided into Pedo-Baptists and Anti-Pedo-Baptists, or Baptists and Pedo-Baptists. The Baptists believe only in *adult* baptism; while Pedo-Baptists believe also in *infant* baptism. Some Pedo-Baptists are *immersionists:* and, *visa versa,* some Baptists are *affusionists*. In other words, some who think *infants* ought to be baptized, believe that *immersion* is the scriptural mode of water baptism; while others who think *adults,* only, ought to be baptized, believe that *affusion* is the scriptural mode of administration. In the absence of better names, we will just call them *Pedo-immersionists* and *Bapto-affusionists*. But we are after the *scriptural subjects* of water baptism now.

Adult Baptism.

Adults who exercise *repentance* toward God, *faith* in Christ and receive *spiritual baptism,* are *scriptural* subjects for water baptism. These are the only conditions upon which we are authorized to baptize adults.

First test. Repentance is necessary. John baptized with water unto *repentance:* he preached and baptized with the baptism of *repentance;* and refused to baptize the Pharisees and Sadducees for want of evidence of *repentance;* saying, Bring forth therefore fruits meet for *repentance.* Peter demanded *repentance* before baptism on the day of Pentecost. "Repent and be baptized," is the royal edict. Therefore *repentance* is a condition to water baptism.

Second test. Faith is also a necessity. Repentance and *faith* are inseparably connected. They are parts of one and the same act of the soul. Repentance in its completion necessarily ends in *faith.* They are parts of the *one step* that takes us out of a state of sin into a state of grace—out of a lost, into a saved state. When one is expressed the other is always implied: hence they are used inter-changably as the conditions of salvation. John told his subjects that they should *believe* on Christ Jesus. Paul and Silas required the jailer to *believe* on the Lord Jesus Christ before they baptized him. And Philip demanded that the Ethiopean eunuch should *believe with all his heart* before he would baptize him. "If thou believest with all thine heart, thou mayest" be baptized, is Heaven's wise decree. Therefore *faith* is also a condition to water baptism.

Third test. Spiritual baptism is *absolutely* essential. Repentance and faith are followed, *instantly*, by the *baptism of the Spirit.* "He that believeth and is *(immediately)* baptized *(with the Holy Ghost)* shall be saved." The apostles did not baptize on the day of Pentecost until after the people had been baptized with the Spirit. The Holy Ghost fell on Cornelius and his company, and, though the first Gentile converts, Peter, who held the keys to the kingdom of heaven, regarded it as satisfactory evidence of their qualification for water baptism, unlocked the doors of the visible church, commanded them to be baptized in the name of the Lord and received them at once into christian fellowship with the Jews. We hope you have followed this line of test argument. Water baptism is conditioned upon *repentance;* repentance *must* end in *faith;* faith is *instantly* followed by *spiritual baptism*, and this qualifies the adult for membership in the visible kingdom, and makes him a *scriptural* subject for water baptism.

INFANT BAPTISM.

All infants of christan parents are *scriptural* subjects for water baptism.

Plea first. Parents are the *divinely* appointed guardians of their children. A guardian, under civil law, represents and acts for his ward. So parents, under ecclesiastical law, legitimately represent and act for their children. It is not only the privilege, but also the bounden duty of all christian parents to dedicate their children, while in infancy, to God. If they do so in the proper spirit, and train them up in the way they should go, they may claim the fulfillment of the precious promise, which is to them and their children, and will receive the divine blessing; for "when they are old they will not depart from it." In fact, all parents are under moral obligations to come to Christ, bring their children and place them, *tenderly* and *affectionately*, in the arms of his *mystical* body, where they can be brought up in the fear, nurture and admonition of the Lord. Suffer the little children to come unto me, and forbid them not: for of such is the kingdom of God, said Jesus, in his displeasure, to his disciples when they rebuked those parents who brought unto him "young children" and "also infants" that he might touch them. "And he took them in his arms, put his hands upon them, and blessed them." Parents are subjects of Christ's visible kingdom. Their children are born into this kingdom; and are *naturally*, and *necessarily*, subjects of its King.

They are Christ's, and members of his visible kingdom, because their parents are. These "children are a heritage of the Lord." All agree, that every member of the visible church *is, or ought to be* baptised. Consequently, the infant children, of all christian parents, *are entitled to* and *ought* to receive water baptism.

Plea second. As a rule, water baptism is a blessing to children. It needs only to be the seal of *true* covenant relationship between God and the parent, and the blessing will follow; good will result to the child. For God will not only visit the iniquity of fathers upon their children: the Lord will also remember his *righteous covenants* with parents, to their children's children, even to the third and fourth generations, But you ask; what good does it do the infant to baptize it? We might just as pertinently ask; what good did it do babies eight days old to circumcise them? We answer both questions at once. All the good that this covenant relationship has in store for them. Paul says, "much every way." But *how much*, Heaven only knows. Therefore infants of believing parents are *scriptural* subjects of, and ought to be brought into covenant relationship with God, through the ordinance of water baptism.

Plea third. Household baptisms furnish a strong presumptive plea in favor of infant baptism. The Gentiles were usually proselyted to the Jewish faith by whole families. So they were frequently converted to Christianity, in the days of the apostles; and the parents, with all the children, *big* and *little*, "the household," the entire family, were baptized with water, and added to the church. Some few of these household baptisms are mentioned by the apostles, without the slightest intimation that the *little ones* were left out in a single instance. Hence "young children" are *scriptural* subjects of, and ought to be brought to Christ, through the ordinance of water baptism.

Plea fourth. There are instances of water baptism on record, where children were *evidently* baptized. We cite *first* the baptism of all Israel. Pharaoh refused at first to let them take their children with them. But Moses said, We will go with our young and with our old, with our sons and with our daughters. So Pharaoh was forced to say, Go ye, serve the Lord; let your little ones also go with you. So Israel journeyed, a mixed multitude, about six hundred thousand men, beside children. And the Lord went before by day in a pillar of a cloud, and by night in a pillar of fire, to give them light. And the children of Israel went down into the midst of the sea, and passed over on dry ground; "the clouds poured out water," and they "were all baptized unto Moses in the cloud and in the sea." Here is a *clear* case of infant baptism by the wholesale. Therefore infants, "little ones," are *scriptural subjects* of water baptism, Anti-Pedo-Baptists to the contrary notwithstanding.

We cite, in the *second* place, the baptism, by John, of "Jerusalem, and all the region round about Jordan." Matthew *evidently* meant the inhabitants of these places: among whom were men, women and children. And any rule that would exclude *the children* because they are not *particularized,* would also exclude *the women* for the same reason: and any reasoning that would exclude *the women and children*, would just as certainly exclude *the men.* The divine record says, "There went out unto him all the land of Judea, and *they* of Jerusalem and were *all* baptized of him; *all,* ALL, ALL; *men, women* and *children.* Here then is another strong plea for infant baptism; for we cannot infer, as in household baptisms, that there were no small children in Jerusalem, all Judea, and all the region round about Jordan. This would be *most too large an inference*, even for an Anti-Pedo-Baptist of the deepest dye.

John did you baptize all of the inhabitants of these places; men women and children? The sacred record is true; I baptized them *all.* Well, you must have been a strange Baptist I must say. O yes! I have it now, you was a PEDO-BAPTIST! as we Baptists call them now. I suppose I was, for I baptized *with,* not *in* water. I also baptized in the *wilderness,* as well as in *Jordan.* The law, under which I lived, said the people should be *sprinkled,* not *immersed;* and a part of my mission in making ready *a people* prepared for the Lord, was "To turn the hearts of the fathers to the children." Therefore I baptized "all the people," parents, "little ones," and *all,* by sprinkling water upon them, just as Pedo-Baptists do now. I was not called *the Baptist,* because, unlike others, I *immersed* the people, or refused to baptize babies; but simply because I baptized so many of both adults and infants. So I have no objection at all to being called a Pedo-Baptist.

We cite, in the *third* place, the babtism of the three thousand on the day of Pentecost. Peter preached a powerful sermon. The people were deeply convicted and asked, what they should do. Peter answered, "Repent, and be baptized *every one of you,"* big, little, old and young: "for the promise is unto *you* and *your children."* "Then they that gladly received his word were baptized: and the same day there were added unto them about three thousand souls," men, women and children. "And the Lord added unto the church daily such as should be saved." Here is the fulfillment of the promise of prophecy to the church. In the midst of her desolation Zion said, The Lord hath forsaken me, and my Lord hath forgotten me. The Lord answered, Behold, I have graven thee upon the palms of my hands, thy children shall make haste. Sing, O heavens, and be joyful, O earth; for the Lord hath comforted his people. Zion—Who hath begotten me these, seeing I have lost my children, and am desolate, a captive, and removing too and fro? and who hath brought up these? Behold I was left alone; these, where had they been? The Lord—Behold, I will lift up my hand to the Gentiles, and set up my standard to the people: and they shall bring thy sons in their arms, and thy daughters shall be carried upon their shoulders, and I will save thy children; and all flesh shall know that I, the Lord am thy Saviour and thy Redeemer, the mighty one of Jacob."

This is in perfect harmony with the great commission, Go ye therefore, and teach all nations, baptizing *them* (that is the nations, which are composed of men, women and children) in the name of the Father, and of the Son, and of the Holy Ghost; teaching them (the parents, and through the parents the children) to observe all things whatsoever I have commanded you: and lo, I am with you alway, even unto the end of the world.

Plea fifth. Water baptism, under the new, is analogous to, if it does not come in lieu of circumcision under the old dispensation. Circumcision, for males only, was well adapted to an age in which women were held in slavish subjection to their *tyranical lords*. But water baptism, for males and females, is equally well adapted to an age in which woman's worth and true nobility are ever recognized. Circumcision sustained the same relation to the law, that baptism does to the gospel. But true circumcision is that of the heart, while outer circumcision is but its sign, and represents the removing of sin by cutting off. Then the essential baptism is that of the Spirit, and water baptism is but its sign, denoting the removal of sin by washing away. Infants were circumcised under the law. If it did them any good whatever, then the law was more gracious than is the gospel, if it denies them water baptism. But this is not the case. Circumcision was a gracious institution, and "profitted much every way." But the Gospel dispensation is one in which grace abounds, and both adults and infants enjoy greater privileges than under the law dispensation. Infants were circumcised and saved, without faith, under the law. Can the gospel be less gracious, and deny them salvation and water baptism? *Never!* For, if it does, then our children are not as well provided for under the gospel, as were the children of the Jews under the law. The new covenant, as well as the old, includes the children. Therefore they are *scriptural* subjects, and graciously entitled to all the benefits and immunities growing out of water baptism.

Plea sixth. The testimony of the fathers in favor of infant baptism is most conclusive. Origen, the great historian, said "they obtained the custom of baptizing infants from the apostles." Cyprian said, "Sixty-six Bishops being convened in a council at Carthage, having the question referred to them, whether infants might be baptized before they were eight days old, decided unanimously that no infant is to be prohibited from the benefit of baptism, although but just born." St. Augustine, referring to infant baptism, said this "doctrine is held by the whole church, not instituted by councils, but always retained." We might add the testimony of Jerome, Crysostom, Ambrose, and in fact, of nearly all the Christian fathers:

but we will close with that of Pelagius who said, "Men slander me, as if I denied the sacriment of baptism to infants. I never heard of any, not even the most impious heritic, who denied baptism to infants." Dr. Wall, of highest ecclesiastical authority, says, "Infant baptism was never called in question until the Twelfth century." Then infants are entitled to, and should be baptized *with* water.

Plea seventh. Infants were members of the visible kingdom under the old, and there is not even an intimation that they were to be denied membership under the new dispensation. Where prejudice has not dethroned reason, innocent infancy, in the visible church, is "like apples of gold in pictures of silver." But Anti-Pedo-Baptists say the old, was but a *type* of the new church. If we admit it they gain nothing; for the anti-type must agree with the type. If the metalic type read, *infant membership* and *infant baptism*, so will its anti-type. There *must be* an agreement between *type* and *anti-type*. But if a "new church" was organized on the day of Pentecost, its membership was made up of Jews; for it was eight years before the first Gentile family was admitted. We submit the question then; if their children were to be excluded under the reign of grace, after enjoying church relationship for two thousand years, would not something have been said to that effect? and if rejected, after being included in the promises of the gospel, would not their parents have stubbornly revolted against such an unnatural, not to say unjust, procedure?

We now submit five questions, relative to infant membership and baptism; and will answer them in *unwrested* scriptures, which we trust will settle, at once and forever, in your minds, the subject of infant baptism.

First question. Was Christ called *a shepherd?* Awake, O sword against my shepherd, saith the Lord of hosts: smite the shepherd, and the sheep shall be scattered: and I will turn my hand (in mercy) upon the little ones. And it shall come to pass, saith the Lord, two parts therein shall be cut off and die; but the third shall be left therein. And I will refine them as silver is refined, and will try them as gold is tried: I will say, It is my people: and they shall say, The Lord is my God. Christ said, I am the good shepherd: the good shepherd giveth his life for the sheep. I am the good shepherd, and know my sheep, and am known of mine: and I lay down my life for the sheep. And other sheep I have, which are not of this fold; them also I must bring, and they shall hear my voice; and there shall be one fold, and one shepherd. Peter said, to the strangers to whom he directed his first epistle, For ye were as sheep going astray; but are now returned unto the Shepherd and Bishop of your souls. Paul in his benediction upon the Hebrews said, Now the God of peace, that brought again from the dead our Lord Jesus, that GREAT SHEPHERD of the sheep, through the blood of the everlasting covenant, make you perfect through Jesus Christ; to whom be glory forever and ever, Amen. And when the CHIEF SHEPHERD shall appear, ye shall receive a crown of glory that fadeth not away. Christ then *was*, and *is a shepherd*.

Second question. Was Christ's visible kingdom, or church, called a flock? The Psalmist said, O, God, thou ledest thy people like a flock by the hand of Moses and Aaron. And again, He made his own people to go forth like sheep, and guided them in the wilderness like a flock. Christ said to his disciples, Fear not, *little flock;* for it is the Father's good pleasure to give you the kingdom. Paul said, to the elders of Ephesus, Take heed therefore unto yourselves and to *all the flock*, over the which the Holy Ghost hath made you overseers, to feed the church of God, which he hath purchased with his own blood. For I know this, that after my departing shall grevious wolves enter in among you, not sparing *the flock*. Peter said, in a general exhortation to the elders of the visible kingdom, Feed *the flock* of God, which is among you, taking the oversight thereof, not by constraint, but willingly; not for filthy luchre, but of a ready mind; neither as being lords over God's heritage, but being ensamples to *the flock*. These answers settle the question. Christ's visible church is called A FLOCK.

Third question. Are there any lambs in Christ's flock? Isaiah, in prophecy, said of Christ, He shall feed his flock like a shepherd: he shall gather *the lambs* with his arm, and carry them in his bosom. Zechariah said, Smite the shepherd, and the sheep (flock) shall be scattered: and I will turn mine hand (in blessings) upon the *little ones*. Then there are LAMBS in Christ's flock.

Fourth question. Who are the *lambs* in Christ's flock? The disciples said unto Jesus, Who is the greatest in the kingdom of heaven? And Jesus called a *little child* unto him, and set him in the midst of them, and said, Verily I say unto you, Except ye be converted, and become as *little children,* ye shall not (in reality) enter into the kingdom of heaven. Whosoever therefore shall humble himself as this *little child,* the same is the greatest in the kingdom of heaven. Then were brought unto him *little children*, that he should put his hands on them, and pray: and his disciples rebuked them. But Jesus said, Suffer *little children*, and forbid them not, to come unto me: for of such is the kingdom of heaven. And he laid his hands on them and departed thence. And they brought *young children* to him, that he should touch them: and his disciples rebuked those that brought them. But when Jesus saw it, he was much displeased, and said unto them, Suffer the *little children* to come unto me, and forbid them not: for of such is the kingdom of God. Verily I say unto you, Whosoever shall not receive the kingdom of God as a *little child* shall in no wise enter therein. Then, the *lambs* of Christ's flock, that he gathered in his arm and carried in his bosom, and *the little ones* among his sheep, upon whom he turned his hand so lovingly, were *the little children, the young children* and also *the infant children* that Jesus, the tender shepherd took in his arms of affection and blessed so fondly. These *lambs* are the *babies* out of whose mouths praise was perfected when they cried, at his triumphal entrance into Jerusalem, Hosanna to the son of David: Hosanna in the highest.

Fifth question. Is it the will of the good

shepherd, that these lambs of his flock should be *baptized?* There is a *real*, and also a *ministerial*, or *ceremonial* sanctification taught in the Bible. The *real* sanctification is by spiritual baptism. Proof of which is found in the following passages; Elect according to the fore knowledge of God the Father, through sanctification of the Spirit, unto obedience and sprinkling of the blood of Jesus Christ. Because God hath from the beginning chosen you to salvation through sanctification of the Spirit and belief of the truth. The *ceremonial* sanctification is by water baptism. Proof of which is found in the following passage; Husbands, love your wives, even as Christ also loved *the church*, and gave himself for it; that he might *sanctify* and cleanse it with *the washing of water* by the word. Here are the two sanctifications, by the two baptisms. But the question is; does Christ will the *ceremonial* sanctification, which is by water baptism, of the children of the church? Let Joel answer this question in his prophesy referring to both the *ceremonial* and *spiritual* sanctification of the remnant of the church on the day of Pentecost. Blow the trumpet in Zion, *sanctify* a fast, call a solemn assembly: gather the people, *sanctify the congregation*, assemble the elders, *gather the children*, and *those that suck the breasts :* let the bridegroom go forth of his chamber, and the bride out of her closet. Then will the Lord pity his people. And it shall come to pass afterward, that I will pour out my spirit upon all flesh; and your sons and your daughters shall prophecy, your old men shall dream dreams, your young men shall see visions: and also upon the servants and upon the handmaids in those days will I pour out my Spirit. There it is, just as it was at the Red Sea, the *ceremonial* sanctification, by water baptism, of *the little children, even those that suck the breasts.* We hope you have followed this unbroken chain of argument in our last plea for infant baptism. Christ is *a shepherd;* the visible church is *his flock;* it contains *lambs;* they are *little children,* infants, *those that suck the breasts,* and it is the will of Christ that *these little ones be baptized with water.* Therefore *the infants* of all christian parents are *scriptural* subjects of water baptism.

The Kingdom of God.

CHAPTER IX.

The Spiritual Church.

The spiritual, and carnal church are not identical. One is visible, the other invisible; one natural, the other supernatural; one organic and the other inorganic. The membership then, of this spiritual kingdom, is spiritual, invisible and inorganic. It is composed of the *souls,* or *spirits* of all christians. These spirits are invisible, and therefore can not be organized. This kingdom has none but a spiritual membership. For Christ said, Except a man be born again he cannot see the kingdom of God.

We distinguish things by their differences, not by their points of resemblance. There is this difference between the visible and invisible church—the kingdom of heaven and the kingdom of God. In the one we have the good and the bad, the pure and the vile of earth, all in, visible, corrupt organization: while in the other we have nothing that defileth, or maketh unclean; nothing but the redeemed spirits of the just, made perfect through the blood of the everlasting covenant. "For flesh and blood can not inherit the kingdom of God."

The fountain head of this great spiritual kingdom is found in a triune God: God in the persons of the Father, Son and Holy Ghost. There is trinity in almost every thing around us. Trinity in nature, trinity in man, trinity in life, trinity in death, trinity in the church and trinity in God. With reference to this world, this triune God established this spiritual kingdom in the heart of the first believing soul of our fallen race. Whether that was Adam, Eve, or Abel, we know not. But, here we find the spiritual kingdom in its incipiency. It is very small: fills but one soul with joy and gladness. "It is like a grain of mustard seed, which a man took and cast into his garden; and it grew and waxed a great tree, and the fowls of the air lodged in the branches of it." So the kingdom of God established—the seed of God sown, in a single heart, sprang up, began to grow, and spread from heart to heart, as it passed on down through the fleeting centuries, ever widening and deepening, as it swept grandly on, in its majestic march, until it numbered its subjects by thousands, and multiplied thousands, even under the old dispensation.

Noah, a preacher of righteousness, had an interest in this kingdom. Abraham, Isaac and Jacob were all identified with this spiritual kingdom. All of the patriarchs, prophets, priests and kings, who were holy men of God, were also humble subjects of this great spiritual kingdom. And all who ate of that spiritual food, and drank of that spiritual Rock, which followed the visible church through the wilderness, were recipients of the blessings of the kingdom of God. John the Baptist, who was filled with the Holy Ghost from his mother's womb, was thus early born of the Spirit and had a special and abiding interest in the kingdom of God. To this spiritual kingdom belonged all of the *true* Israel of God, with the *many* who are to come from the East, West, North and South and sit down, with Abraham, Isaac and Jacob, in the kingdom of ultimate glory. God has never been left without a *true Israel* since the establishment of his kingdom in the world. Elijah thought at one time that he alone was left; but God informed him that there were *seven thousand,* in Israel, who had not bowed the knee to Baal. So this spiritual kingdom has always had its consecrated membership; *its loyal, true, devoted, loving hearts.* It has ever been "a chosen generation, a royal priesthood, an holy nation, a peculiar people," offering spiritual sacrifices, holy and acceptable unto God.

We must not lose sight of the fact that Christ is verily God; and that he is the KING of this spiritual kingdom. "For this ye know, that no whoremonger, nor unclean person, nor covetous man, who is an idolator, hath any inheritance in the kingdom of *Christ*, and of God; who hath delivered us from the power of darkness, and hath translated us into the kingdom of *his dear Son.*"

We have already shown that this spiritual kingdom was united with the visible kingdom at the ushering in of the Gospel dispensation. This important union, under Christ, the legitimate heir to both kingdoms, constituted *a dual kingdom* of increased power and efficiency in the world. The spiritual kingdom is now more *permanently* established. It has taken a deeper, stronger hold upon the hearts and consciences of the people than ever before. The kingdom of God has come with *power* and *great glory*. Evidences of increased power, and manifestations of divine glory, in this dual kingdom, are to be seen on every hand. The deaf hear; the dumb talk; the blind see; the dead live, and multiplied thousands are being born of the Spirit, filled with the Holy Ghost, and added to the visible kingdom such as shall be saved.

This dual kingdom is the world's great "beacon light." Christ said of her, Ye are the light of the world. And as she stands, in her loveliness, upon the strands of time, she ever beckons the world onward and upward, with her beams of light and floods of glory, breaking in upon the shores of eternity. She is most emphatically the grand "Light House" of the world. Her light shines by day and by night. In her, because she is in God, there is no darkness at all; but her light *so* shines that others seeing her good works are constrained to glorify God. And the burden of her, *heart-moving* and *soul-stirring,* song is, "Now is come salvation, and strength and the kingdom of our God, and the power of his Christ." Now in fulfillment of her heaven-born mission, she is sending the messengers of life and light "throughout every city and village, preaching and showing the glad tidings of the kingdom of God.

This spiritual kingdom is of divine origin. Christ said of it, before he took charge of the visible church; but now is my kingdom not of this world. It is from heaven, though established in this world. "The kingdom of God cometh not with observation." It can not be seen, because spiritual. "Neither shall they say, Lo here, or Lo there, for (it is not located as are the kingdoms of this world) behold, the kingdom of God is within you," *invisibly* located in the soul. The origin, spirit and mission of this kingdom, are all heavenly. Hence it bestows the richest temporal, as well as spiritual blessings on the world. "Seek ye first the kingdom of God, and his righteousness; and all these things shall be added into you." But its true dominion is in the soul. Here it reigns supreme. "For the kingdom of God is not meat and drink; but righteousness, and peace, and joy in the Holy Ghost." Wherever you find a soul full of *righteousness, peace,* and *joy* in the *Holy Ghost;* whether in time, or eternity; whether in this or the eternal world, there you will find established this spiritual kingdom—the kingdom of God.

This spiritual kingdom can not be inherited by the unrighteous, effeminate, abusers of themselves with mankind, nor by thieves, covetous, drunkers, revilers or extortioners. Not one of these characters, as such, can enter or enjoy this kingdom: for they are destitute of righteousness, and this is a kingdom of righteousness; destitute of peace, and this is a kingdom of peace; destitute of joy in the Holy Ghost, and this is *preeminently* a kingdom of joy, unspeakable and full of glory, shed abroad in our hearts by the Holy Ghost which is given unto us. But thousands of these characters, cleansed from all their filthiness, washed, sanctified, and justified in the name of Jesus and by the Spirit of our God, have entered into the enjoyment of this spiritual kingdom, with sweetest assurance of joys eternal and pleasures which are lasting and forevermore. For this kingdom embraces all, of every age and clime, who are united, by the Spirit, to Christ as their divine Head: and also proffers blessings untold, to all who will throw off the shackles of sin, don the robe of Christ's righteousness, confessing allegiance to him as King of kings and Lord of lords.

This spiritual kingdom is a kingdom of power. Though invisible, there is latent power in it sufficient to move the world. For the kingdom of God is not in word, but in *power,* said the Saviour. The kingdom of God is like leaven hid in meal; it was small at first, barely discernable; but it has been constantly working, gradually growing, and ever increasing in vital power, as the ages melted away, until its divine influence is felt far and near; and it is destined, sooner or later, to leaven the whole mass of mankind, the world over. For when we note the recent changes of attitude, among many heathen nations, toward the gospel; and the wide-spread interest, and deep-seated spirituality that pervades the army of the Lord in Christian lands, we are forced to the conclusion, that truly, the kingdom of God is coming with *matchless power* and *transcendent glory.* We see that the leaven is still working, and as christians we can but rejoice at the many evidences, of the final triumph of this spiritual kingdom, which are constantly floating to the service in the form of gospel victories. Since its union with the visible, into one grand dual kingdom, in which the head, heart, and hand, of the Lord's great army, are united to do battle for the Master, marvelous indeed have been the spread, growth, progress and conquests of the kingdom of God in the world. Thus the church militant moves steadily on from conquest to victory, toward the day of her final, and universal triumph over satan's kingdom.

This spiritual, is a kingdom difficult of entrance. Its "strait and narrow gate" is faithfully guarded day, and night, against intruders. To enter it requires the supreme affections of the heart. The uppermost seat in our affections must be consecrated to Christ. We must love God with all the soul—with supreme love. If any thing gets between us and the Saviour it *must be* removed. The more we love it, the more difficult it will be to remove it. O, how difficult it is for those who have their affections centered on the things of this world, to lose sight of all, for a look at the cross! It is seldom we can induce them to make the necessary sacrifice. "How hardly shall they that have riches enter into the kingdom of God." Oh! how few of us, at heart, prefer Christ and the cross to the pleasures, riches and honors of this life! How few are willing, if need be, to forsake all for Christ and his cause! And yet nothing short of such consecration to the cross will suffice. If we have sins, as dear as the right hand, we must cut them off; or if, dearer than the right eye, we must pluck them out; for "we must through much tribulation, enter into the kingdom of God."

But once in this kingdom, and we are saved. We only enter it through a spiritual birth—being born of God. We can enter, in no other way. "Except a man be born of the Spirit he *can not enter into* the kingdom of God." But once in this kingdom, the only *concievable way* to get out, since none can pluck us out, is to *sin* out. But this we *can not* do, because we are born of God. We can not sin *wilfully, meanly,* or *maliciously;* and, for sin in no other sense, would God throw us out of his kingdom. "Whosoever is born of God doth not commit sin; for his seed remaineth in him; and he *can not* sin, because he is born of God." It is contrary to his renewed nature to sin, save through *ignorance, weakness of the flesh,* and *the temptations* of the devil; hence he *can not* sin himself out of, but remains in the kingdom of God forever and forever—during time and throughout boundless eternity.

This dual kingdom of Christ will know no end. It is an *everlasting* kingdom." The implements of war will all be converted into the implements of agriculture: the conquests of the world will be made with the weapons of truth and love; the heathen will be given him for an inheritance and the uttermost parts of the earth for a possession, and the kingdoms of this world will all become the kingdoms of our Lord and of his Christ. Then cometh the end of time, the resurrection of the dead, the change of the living, the reunion of the glorified souls and bodies of the entire membership of this dual kingdom, constituting a truer, more intimate and glorious union of the visible and spiritual in the glorified kingdom, which Christ now delivers up to God even the Father: and in its glorified state this everlasting kingdom sweeps grandly on down through the sycles of eternity paralled with a triune God, who is all in all. Thus the dual kingdom will be lost eternally in the glorified kingdom, where all will be happiness and heaven.

The Father's Kingdom.

CHAPTER X.

THE GLORIFIED CHURCH.

The glorified church will be a grand consummation of the visible and spiritual kingdom—a continuation, eternally, of the *dual* kingdom. We have already seen, that Christ's everlasting kingdom, after it has attained to universal dominion, broken in pieces all other kingdoms, and filled the whole earth with its glory, is to be *submerged,* or *lost* in the glorified kingdom of the Father. After the great redemption work is consummated the kingdom of boundless grace will be swallowed up in the kingdom of ultimate and eternal glory.

There will be two component parts in this glorified kingdom. The subjects and the place occupied. It will be located in heaven. The place is already prepared, and spoken of as a kingdom. "Come ye blessed of my Father, inherit *the kingdom* prepared for you from the foundation of the world." This will be the king's welcome plaudit to the glorified church, when he transfers her from earth to heaven. The judgment passed, "the righteous saved, the wicked damned and God's eternal government approved," Christ, with the happy subjects of this kingdom, and his shining retinue of angels, will take up his triumphal march across the fields of light toward the city of the New Jerusalem. Grand, glorious and triumphant indeed will be the transfer of this glorified kingdom—the heavenly march of this victorious army, as it speeds on in triumph over the plains of light toward the Blessed City. Listen! Oh, ye lovers of marshal music, to the grand chorus that bows the lofty heavens, to lend a listening ear to its melting strains * * * music, far, sweeter than the chorus of the morning stars that sang together at creation's birth * * * music, tuned to the lay of immortal eloquence, and sung, in raptures of sweetest melody, as the heavenly hosts sweep on triumphantly toward the New Jerusalem— Lift up your heads, O ye gates; and be ye lift up, ye everlasting doors; and the King of glory shall come in. Who is this King of glory? inquire the keepers of the gates. The Lord strong and mighty, the Lord mighty in battle, is the responce. Then the grand chorus salutes their ears again—Lift up your heads, O ye gates; even lift them up, ye everlasting doors; and the King of glory shall come in.

Who is this King of glory? The Lord of hosts, he is the King of glory. The pearly gates fly open, the Conqueror, with his ransomed hosts, passes in with triumph: and the inquiry comes, Who are these? The answer is given back; These are the *glorified ones;* they who came up through many tribulations have washed their robes and made them white in the blood of the Lamb. And the Eternal City rings with the loud hosannahs and sweet halleluiahs of welcome to the King and his victorious army—the subjects of the glorified kingdom.

This glorified kingdom will know no sin; no death. Heaven, with all its lovliness, once had its revolutions; with all its enjoyment, once knew discontent; with all its harmony, once felt the dire effects of rebellion. But the sound of war will be heard no more in all the vast dominions of this glorified kingdom. Sin and death will never more make their inroads upon the happy subjects of this sinless and immortalized kingdom. Sin is the source of all our misery—the barrier to universal happiness. It is the author of all our delusive hopes, and hails with delight our sadest disappointments. Every arriving moment comes ladened with trouble, affliction, bereavement and death, all in consequence of sin. *Inheritance? Sin has none.* It is a worthless vagabond, *crouching* and *cowering* beneath the lash of divine justice, and is doomed to eternal bankruptcy. It has no reward for its servants, save the pleasures of sin for a season, and in the end eternal death. "For the wages of sin is death." We do not hesitate to stigmatize sin as the *deadly upas tree* of the world, that has thrown its *withering, blasting, blackening, damning shadows* over all the nations of the earth, until the world travailleth in pain even till now; and her sons and daughters everywhere are groaning under the burden of guilt, misery and woe, a *dire* legacy to them by sin bequeathed. Happy day! glorious kingdom! that will deliver us, *once* and *forever*, from the *reign* of sin and the *dominion* of death.

This glorified kingdom will be one of truth and love: a kingdom of perfect order, peace, knowledge, and righteousness, where countless millions of glorified ones will live eternally without sin. It will be *a vast* and *glorious* empire, where happy millions will live in perfect obedience to their King, to whom allegiance is infinite delight. There the night of ignorance will cast no *withering shadow* over happy homes; but the blest inhabitants will be robed in garments of unfading light, bask in the sunshine of its glory and enjoy its boundless riches forever more. Thrice happy the subjects of such a glorious kingdom!

This glorified, will be a kingdom of *inconcievable joy* and *blessedness*. It will be a garden of pleasures, full of beauty and loveliness. It will furnish all that the glorified can possibly desire; riches without want, health without sickness, pleasure without pain, joy without sorrow, light without darkness and life without death. Christians will have administered unto them, either a meager, or an abundant entrance into this everlasting kingdom of the Father. We will enter either with a starless, or a star-bespangled crown into the kingdom of ultimate glory. Every capacity will be full to overflowing however; and every child of the kingdom perfect in his sphere. "Then shall the righteous shine forth as the sun in the kingdom of their Father, and they that turn many to righteousness, as the stars forever and ever." We know, comparatively speaking, but little either of the employment, or blessedness, of the subjects of this glorified kingdom. But the Scriptures abound in the most beautiful and impressive images that nature and art could possibly furnish, to illustrate its happiness and prove its divine reality. They speak of this kingdom as an endless inheritance—a better country, flowing with rivers of pleasure, shaded by trees of life, full of rapturous songs and rich with robes and crowns, feasting mirth, treasures and eternal triumphs. They teach us that the righteous shall *actually* appear, in this kingdom, in Christ's glory—with bodies like unto his *glorified* body, and there dwell forever in the *wholly reconciled presence* of the Father. But the half has not been told. For eye hath not seen, nor ear heard, neither hath it entered into the heart of man to concieve of the *unspeakable joy* and *eternal blessedness* that awaits his glorified children, in the Father's kingdom.

This glorified, will be a kingdom of *boundless* and *endless* glory. The visible kingdom was *glorious;* the dual kingdom *excelled in glory;* but *the glorified kingdom* will be *full of infinite* and *eternal glory:* Its happy subjects will be changed from *glory to glory,* in the image of the Lord, until they have *fully realized the far more exceeding and eternal weight of glory,* to be found and enjoyed in the Father's kingdom of *ultimate* and *eternal glory.* In this glorious kingdom heart will answer to heart, in the sweetest responses of love, and the dearest interests and most sacred associations, gather around an immortal life, that runs parallel with God and eternity. Here countless millions of happy children will love the same kind, heavenly Father, receive from his bountiful hand the same needed blessings and share through all eternity the same rich and glorious inheritance. Blessed kingdom! where sickness will never come, painful partings will be known no more, but in which all the *great family* of the Father shall live on and on through the long cycles of eternity, in all the bloom and vigor of immortal youth.

Dear reader, in Christ, this kingdom *so great, so beautiful, so good* and *so full of infinite and eternal glory,* is to be *our* kingdom. And we imagine there will be *great joy, boundless glory,* that multiplied millions of happy voices will unite in a mighty song of triumph, that will roll in undying anthems around the eternal throne, when all of his *dear glorified children* are *forever housed* in the Father's kingdom.

REMARKS.

First. We sold two hundred copies of this little book before it left the press.

Second. It sells itself. Its title, size, style and price will sell it anywhere.

Third. Price, in leatherette binding, twenty-five cents; in substantial cloth binding, fifty cents; in the *most handsome* morocco binding, gilt-edged, one dollar per copy.

Fourth. On all orders, amounting to over one dollar, we will give a reduction of twenty-five per cent.

Fifth. All orders addressed, at any time, to the author, Rev. L. McWherter, Union City, Tenn., will reach him and be filled *promptly.*

ERRATA.

Page 13. "Penticost" should read, Pentecost.
Page 14. "Penticost" should read, Pentecost.
Page 21. "In order to," should be omitted.

CONTENTS.

CHAPTER.   **PAGE.**

I.   The Origin of the Visible Church.   1

II.   The Identity of the Visible Church.   13

III.   The Identity of the Visible Church.   25

IV.   The Perpetuity of the Visible Church. 37

V.   The Ordinances of the Visible Kingdom 49

VI.   The Design of Water Baptism.   60

VII.   The Mode of Water Baptism.   75

VIII.   The Subjects of Water Baptism.   94

IX.   The Spiritual Church.   112

X.   The Glorified Church.   122

www.ingramcontent.com/pod-product-compliance
Lightning Source LLC
Chambersburg PA
CBHW022133160426
43197CB00009B/1264